LAST DAY

EVENTS

Facing Earth's Final Crisis

Compiled from the Writings

of

Ellen G. White

Pacific Press® Publishing Association
Nampa, Idaho
Oshawa, Ontario, Canada

Copyright © 1992 by
Pacific Press® Publishing Association
Printed in United States of America
All Rights Reserved

**Library of Congress Cataloging-in-Publication
Data:**

White, Ellen Gould Harmon, 1827-1915.
  Last day events: facing earth's final crisis/compiled
from the writings of Ellen G. White.
        p.   cm.
  Includes index.
  ISBN 13:978-0-8163-1879-7 (hard cover)
  ISBN 10:0-8163-1879-4
  ISBN 13:978-0-8163-1901-5 (paper cover)
  ISBN 10: 0-8163-1901-4
  1. Eschatology. I. Title.
BT821.W585   1992   91-42012
236'.9—dc20   CIP

Abbreviations of Sources

AA	*The Acts of the Apostles*
AH	*The Adventist Home*
1BC	*The Seventh-day Adventist Bible Commentary,* vol. 1 (2BC, etc., for vols. 2-7)
CD	*Counsels on Diet and Foods*
CG	*Child Guidance*
CH	*Counsels on Health*
ChS	*Christian Service*
CL	*Country Living*
CM	*Colporteur Ministry*
CS	*Counsels on Stewardship*
CSW	*Counsels on Sabbath School Work*
COL	*Christ's Object Lessons*
CT	*Counsels to Teachers, Parents, and Students*
CW	*Counsels to Writers and Editors*
DA	*The Desire of Ages*
Ed	*Education*
EGW'88	*The Ellen G. White 1888 Materials*
Ev	*Evangelism*
EW	*Early Writings*
FE	*Fundamentals of Christian Education*
GC	*The Great Controversy Between Christ and Satan*
GCB	*General Conference Bulletin*
GCDB	*General Conference Daily Bulletin*
GH	*The Gospel Herald*
GW	*Gospel Workers*

1SP	*Spirit of Prophecy,* vol. 1
	(2SP etc. for vols. 2-4)
SpT-A	*Special Testimonies, Series A*
SpT-B	*Special Testimonies, Series B*
SR	*The Story of Redemption*
ST	*The Signs of the Times*
SW	*The Southern Work*
1T	*Testimonies for the Church,* vol. 1,
	(2T, etc., for vols. 2-9)
TDG	*This Day With God*
Te	*Temperance*
TM	*Testimonies to Ministers and Gospel Workers*
TMK	*That I May Know Him*
UL	*The Upward Look*

To The Reader

Seventh-day Adventists believe they have been especially called of God to proclaim the good news of Christ's soon coming to a confused and dying world. "Great pains," Ellen White wrote, "should be taken to keep this subject before the people" (FE 336). In her book *The Great Controversy Between Christ and Satan*, she graphically outlined the grand and dreadful events of the future. There is no other book like it. *Maranatha,* a 1976 book compiled from her writings, also deals with the fulfillment of last-day Bible prophecies.

As a further effort to "keep this subject before the people," we have prepared the present volume, *Last Day Events.* Many of the citations in this book have been drawn from previously published Ellen White sources, but a fair percentage of the materials have never before been published. While we have not included all of Ellen White's statements on earth's closing events, we have endeavored to include the most significant ones.

At the close of each excerpt, we have provided a source credit as well as the date when the passage was written, or a date when it was published during Ellen White's lifetime. We also have included a few footnotes, where we have thought that additional information or explanations would be helpful.

We have attempted to present Ellen White's teachings on end-time events in a logical arrangement.

However, we do not claim that we have listed all future events in the exact order of their occurrence. In a matter of such great importance as the experience of God's people in the days ahead, when everyone will have to stand alone, "as though there were not another person in the world" (7BC 983), it is essential that all Christians have their own convictions, based upon their own study and their own personal relationship with the Lord.

Ellen White declares that "our little world is the lesson book of the universe" (DA 19), and that the invisible world is watching "with inexpressible interest" (PK 148) the closing scenes of this world's history. May we all endeavor to catch something of the significance of earth's climactic events as we view them in their relation to the great controversy between good and evil. And may we share with others the glorious truth that Jesus is coming soon.

Contents

1.

Earth's Last Crisis

Widespread Apprehension About the Future

The present is a time of overwhelming interest to all living. Rulers and statesmen, men who occupy positions of trust and authority, thinking men and women of all classes, have their attention fixed upon the events taking place about us. They are watching the relations that exist among the nations. They observe the intensity that is taking possession of every earthly element and they recognize that something great and decisive is about to take place—that the world is on the verge of a stupendous crisis.—PK 537 (c. 1914).

The calamities by land and sea, the unsettled state of society, the alarms of war, are portentous. They forecast approaching events of the greatest magnitude. The agencies of evil are combining their forces and consolidating. They are strengthening for the last great crisis. Great changes are soon to take place in our world, and the final movements will be rapid ones.—9T 11 (1909).

Troublous Times Soon to Come

The time of trouble, which is to increase until the end, is very near at hand. We have no time to lose. The world is stirred with the spirit of war. The prophecies of the eleventh of Daniel have almost reached their final fulfillment.—RH Nov. 24, 1904.

The time of trouble—trouble such as was not since there was a nation [Dan. 12:1]—is right upon us, and we are like the sleeping virgins. We are to awake and ask the Lord Jesus to place underneath us His everlasting arms, and carry us through the time of trial before us.—3MR 305 (1906).

The world is becoming more and more lawless. Soon great trouble will arise among the nations—trouble that will not cease until Jesus comes.—RH Feb. 11, 1904.

We are on the very verge of the time of trouble, and perplexities that are scarcely dreamed of are before us.—9T 43 (1909).

We are standing on the threshold of the crisis of the ages. In quick succession the judgments of God will follow one another—fire, and flood, and earthquake, with war and bloodshed.—PK 278 (c. 1914).

There are stormy times before us, but let us not utter one word of unbelief or discouragement.—ChS 136 (1905).

God Has Always Warned of Coming Judgments

God has always given men warning of coming judgments. Those who had faith in His message for their time, and who acted out their faith in obedience to His commandments, escaped the judgments that fell upon the disobedient and unbelieving.

The word came to Noah, "Come thou and all thy house into the ark; for thee have I seen righteous before Me." Noah obeyed and was saved. The message came to Lot, "Up, get you out of this place; for the Lord will destroy this city" (Gen. 7:1; 19:14). Lot placed himself under the guardianship of the heavenly messengers and was saved. So Christ's disciples were given warning of the destruction of Jerusalem. Those who watched for the sign of the coming ruin, and fled from the city, escaped the destruction. So now we are given warning of Christ's second coming and of the destruction to fall upon the world. Those who heed the warning will be saved.—DA 634 (1898).

God Has Told Us What to Expect in Our Day

Before His crucifixion the Saviour explained to His disciples that He was to be put to death and to rise again from the tomb, and angels were present to impress His words on minds and hearts.[1] But the disciples were looking for temporal deliverance from the Roman yoke, and they could not tolerate the thought that He in whom all their hopes centered should suffer an ignominious death. The words which

---

1. See Mark 8:31, 32; 9:31; 10:32-34.

they needed to remember were banished from their minds, and when the time of trial came it found them unprepared. The death of Jesus as fully destroyed their hopes as if He had not forewarned them.

So in the prophecies the future is opened before us as plainly as it was opened to the disciples by the words of Christ. The events connected with the close of probation and the work of preparation for the time of trouble, are clearly presented. But multitudes have no more understanding of these important truths than if they had never been revealed.—GC 594 (1911).

Last Day Prophecies Demand Our Attention

I then saw the third angel [Rev. 14:9-11]. Said my accompanying angel, "Fearful is his work. Awful is his mission. He is the angel that is to select the wheat from the tares and seal, or bind, the wheat for the heavenly garner. These things should engross the whole mind, the whole attention."—EW 118 (1854).

We shall have to stand before magistrates to answer for our allegiance to the law of God, to make known the reasons of our faith. And the youth should understand these things.

They should know the things that will come to pass before the closing up of the world's history. These things concern our eternal welfare, and teachers and students should give more attention to them.—6T 128, 129 (1900).

We should study the great waymarks that point out the times in which we are living.—4MR 163 (1895).

Those who place themselves under God's control, to be led and guided by Him, will catch the steady tread of the events ordained by Him to take place.—7T 14 (1902).

We are to see in history the fulfillment of prophecy, to study the workings of Providence in the great reformatory movements, and to understand the progress of events in the marshaling of the nations for the final conflict of the great controversy.—8T 307 (1904).

Study the Books of Daniel and Revelation Especially

There is need of a much closer study of the Word of God; especially should Daniel and the Revelation have attention as never before. . . . The light that Daniel received from God was given especially for these last days.—TM 112, 113 (1896).

Let us read and study the twelfth chapter of Daniel. It is a warning that we shall all need to understand before the time of the end.—15 MR 228 (1903).

The last book of the New Testament scriptures is full of truth that we need to understand.—COL 133 (1900).

The unfulfilled predictions of the book of Revelation are soon to be fulfilled. This prophecy is now to be studied with diligence by the people of God and should be clearly understood. It does not conceal the truth; it clearly forewarns, telling us what will be in the future.—1NL 96 (1903).

The solemn messages that have been given in their order in the Revelation are to occupy the first place in the minds of God's people.—8T 302 (1904).

The Subject Should Be
Kept Before the People

There are many who do not understand the prophecies relating to these days and they must be enlightened. It is the duty of both watchmen and laymen to give the trumpet a certain sound.—Ev 194, 195 (1875).

Let the watchmen now lift up their voice and give the message which is present truth for this time. Let us show the people where we are in prophetic history.—5T 716 (1889).

There is a day that God hath appointed for the close of this world's history: "This gospel of the kingdom shall be preached in all the world for a witness unto all nations; and *then* shall the end come." Prophecy is fast fulfilling. More, much more, should be said about these tremendously important subjects. The day is at hand when the destiny of souls will be fixed forever. . . .

Great pains should be taken to keep this subject before the people. The solemn fact is to be kept not only before the people of the world but before our own churches also, that the day of the Lord will come suddenly, unexpectedly. The fearful warning of the

prophecy is addressed to every soul. Let no one feel
that he is secure from the danger of being surprised.
Let no one's interpretation of prophecy rob you of the
conviction of the knowledge of events which show that
this great event is near at hand.—FE 335, 336 (1895).

Keeping Future Events in Proper Perspective

We are not now able to describe with accuracy the
scenes to be enacted in our world in the future, but this
we do know, that this is a time when we must watch
unto prayer, for the great day of the Lord is at hand.
—2SM 35 (1901).

The mark of the beast is exactly what it has been
proclaimed to be. Not all in regard to this matter is yet
understood nor will it be understood until the unrolling
of the scroll.—6T 17 (1900).

Many will look away from present duties, present
comfort and blessings, and be borrowing trouble in
regard to the future crisis. This will be making a time
of trouble beforehand, and we will receive no grace for
any such anticipated troubles.—3SM 383, 384 (1884).

There is a time of trouble coming to the people of
God, but we are not to keep that constantly before the
people and rein them up to have a time of trouble
beforehand. There is to be a shaking among God's
people, but this is not the present truth to carry to the
churches.—1SM 180 (1890).

2.

Signs of Christ's Soon Return

Our Lord's Great Prophecy

Christ forewarned His disciples of the destruction of Jerusalem and the signs to take place prior to the coming of the Son of man. The whole of the twenty-fourth chapter of Matthew is a prophecy concerning the events to precede this event, and the destruction of Jerusalem is used to typify the last great destruction of the world by fire.—Ms 77, 1899.

Christ upon the Mount of Olives rehearsed the fearful judgments that were to precede His second coming: "Ye shall hear of wars and rumors of wars: . . . Nation shall rise against nation, and kingdom against kingdom: and there shall be famines, and pestilences, and earthquakes, in divers places. All these are the beginning of sorrows" [Matt. 24:6-8]. While these prophecies received a partial fulfillment at the destruction of Jerusalem, they have a more direct application in the last days.—5T 753 (1899).

Signs in the Heavens

At the close of the great papal persecution, Christ declared, the sun should be darkened, and the moon should not give her light. Next, the stars should fall from heaven. And He says, "Learn a parable of the fig tree; When his branch is yet tender, and putteth forth leaves, ye know that summer is nigh: so likewise ye, when ye shall see all these things, know that He is near, even at the doors" (Matt. 24:32, 33, margin).

Christ has given signs of His coming. He declares that we may know when He is near, even at the doors. He says of those who see these signs, "This generation shall not pass, till all these things be fulfilled." These signs have appeared.[1] Now we know of a surety that the Lord's coming is at hand.—DA 632 (1898).

Signs on the Earth

Jesus declares: "There shall be signs in the sun, and in the moon, and in the stars; and upon the earth distress of nations" (Luke 21:25; Matt. 24:29; Mark 13:24-26; Rev. 6:12-17). Those who behold these harbingers of His coming are to "know that it is near, even at the doors" (Matt. 24:33).—GC 37, 38 (1911).

The nations are in unrest. Times of perplexity are upon us. Men's hearts are failing them for fear of the things that are coming upon the earth. But those who believe in God will hear His voice amid the storm, saying, "It is I; be not afraid."—ST Oct. 9, 1901.

---

1. See *The Great Controversy*, pp. 306-308, 333, 334.

Strange and eventful history is being recorded in the books of heaven—events which it was declared should shortly precede the great day of God. Everything in the world is in an unsettled state.—3MR 313 (1908).

False Prophets

As one of the signs of Jerusalem's destruction, Christ had said, "Many false prophets shall rise, and shall deceive many" [Matt. 24:11]. False prophets did rise, deceiving the people and leading great numbers into the desert. Magicians and sorcerers, claiming miraculous power, drew the people after them into the mountain solitudes. But this prophecy was spoken also for the last days. This sign is given as a sign of the second advent.—DA 631 (1898).

We shall encounter false claims, false prophets will arise, there will be false dreams and false visions, but preach the Word; be not drawn away from the voice of God in His Word.—2SM 49 (1894).

I have been shown many who will claim to be especially taught of God, and will attempt to lead others, and from mistaken ideas of duty they will undertake a work that God has never laid upon them. Confusion will be the result. Let everyone seek God most earnestly for himself that he may individually understand His will.—2SM 72 (1893).

An Experience With a False Prophet

Last night a young man, a stranger to us all, but professing to be a brother from Victoria [Australia], called upon us and asked to see Sister White. It was evening and I declined seeing him. We invited him to remain with us during the night, however, and to take breakfast. After our usual morning worship, as we were about to go to our various employments, this young man arose and with a commanding gesture requested us to sit down. He said, "Have you any hymnbooks? We will sing a hymn, then I have a message to give you." I said, "If you have a message, give it without delay, for we are very much pressed to get off the American mail and have no time to lose." He then began to read something he had written, which stated among other things that the judgment has now begun upon the living. . . .

I listened as he went on and finally said, "My brother, you are not exactly in your right mind. State plainly how your message concerns us. Please let us know at once. Your mind is overstrained, you misapprehend your work. Much that you have said is in accordance with the Bible, and we believe every word of that. But you are overexcited. Please state what you have for us."

Well, he said that we must pack up and move at once to Battle Creek. I asked his reasons, and he responded, "To give this message that the judgment has begun upon the living." I answered him, "The work which the Lord has given us to do is not yet finished. When our work here is completed we are sure the Lord will let us know that it is time for us to move to Battle Creek, instead of teaching you our duty." . . . I left him for Brother Starr to talk with further while I resumed my writing.

He told Brother Starr that when Sister White spoke to him so kindly, and yet with such authority, he began to see that he had made a mistake, that the impressions which had moved him so strongly were not consistent or reasonable. Although our family is large, consisting of ten members, besides three visitors, we decided to have this young man stay with us for a time. We dare not have him go with people who will treat him harshly and condemn him, neither do we want him to repeat his "revelations." We will have him remain for a little time where we can associate with him and if possible lead him in safe, sure paths. —Letter 66, 1894.

Gluttony and Intemperance

Gluttony and intemperance lie at the foundation of the great moral depravity in our world. Satan is aware of this and he is constantly tempting men and women to indulge the taste at the expense of health and even life itself. Eating, drinking, and dressing are made the aim of life with the world. Just such a state of things existed before the Flood. And this state of dissipation is one of the marked evidences of the soon close of this earth's history.—Letter 34, 1875.

The picture which Inspiration has given of the antediluvian world represents too truly the condition to which modern society is fast hastening.—PP 102 (1890).

We know that the Lord is coming very soon. The world is fast becoming as it was in the days of Noah. It is given over to selfish indulgence. Eating and drinking are carried to excess. Men are drinking the poisonous liquor that makes them mad.—Letter 308, 1907.

Deeds of Violence

In the days of Noah the overwhelming majority was opposed to the truth, and enamored with a tissue of falsehoods. The land was filled with violence. War, crime, murder, was the order of the day. Just so will it be before Christ's second coming.—1BC 1090 (1891).

The labor unions are quickly stirred to violence if their demands are not complied with. Plainer and plainer is it becoming that the inhabitants of the world are not in harmony with God. No scientific theory can explain the steady march of evil workers under the generalship of Satan. In every mob wicked angels are at work, rousing men to commit deeds of violence. . . .

The perversity and cruelty of men will reach such a height that God will reveal Himself in His majesty. Very soon the wickedness of the world will have reached its limit and, as in the days of Noah, God will pour out His judgments.—UL 334 (1903).

The terrible reports we hear of murders and robberies, of railway accidents and deeds of violence, tell the story that the end of all things is at hand. Now, just now, we need to be preparing for the Lord's second coming.—Letter 308, 1907.

Wars and Disasters

The tempest is coming and we must get ready for its
fury by having repentance toward God and faith
toward our Lord Jesus Christ. The Lord will arise to
shake terribly the earth. We shall see troubles on all
sides. Thousands of ships will be hurled into the
depths of the sea. Navies will go down, and human
lives will be sacrificed by millions. Fires will break out
unexpectedly and no human effort will be able to
quench them. The palaces of earth will be swept away
in the fury of the flames. Disasters by rail will become
more and more frequent. Confusion, collision, and
death without a moment's warning will occur on the
great lines of travel. The end is near, probation is
closing. Oh, let us seek God while He may be found,
call upon Him while He is near!—MYP 89, 90 (1890).

In the last scenes of this earth's history war will
rage. There will be pestilence, plague and famine. The
waters of the deep will overflow their boundaries.
Property and life will be destroyed by fire and flood.
We should be preparing for the mansions that Christ
has gone to prepare for them that love Him.—Mar 174
(1897).

Great Balls of Fire

Last Friday morning, just before I awoke, a very
impressive scene was presented before me. I seemed
to awake from sleep but was not in my home. From the
windows I could behold a terrible conflagration. Great

balls of fire were falling upon houses, and from these balls fiery arrows were flying in every direction. It was impossible to check the fires that were kindled, and many places were being destroyed. The terror of the people was indescribable. After a time I awoke and found myself at home.—Ev 29 (1906).

I saw an immense ball of fire fall among some beautiful mansions, causing their instant destruction. I heard someone say: "We knew that the judgments of God were coming upon the earth, but we did not know that they would come so soon." Others, with agonized voices, said: "You knew! Why then did you not tell us? We did not know."—9T 28 (1909).

Earthquakes and Floods

The enemy has worked, and he is working still. He is come down in great power, and the Spirit of God is being withdrawn from the earth. God has withdrawn His hand. We have only to look at Johnstown [Pennsylvania]. He did not prevent the devil from wiping that whole city out of existence.[2] And these very things will increase until the close of this earth's history.—1SAT 109 (1889).

The earth's crust will be rent by the outbursts of the elements concealed in the bowels of the earth. These elements, once broken loose, will sweep away the treasures of those who for years have been adding to

---

2. On May 31, 1889, an estimated 2,200 people lost their lives in the Johnstown flood when a dam broke after many days of heavy rains.

their wealth by securing large possessions at starvation prices from those in their employ. And the religious world, too, is to be terribly shaken, for the end of all things is at hand.—3MR 208 (1891).

The time is now come when one moment we may be on solid earth, the next the earth may be heaving beneath our feet. Earthquakes will take place when least expected.—TM 421 (1896).

In fires, in floods, in earthquakes, in the fury of the great deep, in calamities by sea and by land, the warning is given that God's Spirit will not always strive with men.—3MR 315 (1897).

Before the Son of man appears in the clouds of heaven everything in nature will be convulsed. Lightning from heaven uniting with the fire in the earth will cause the mountains to burn like a furnace and pour out their floods of lava over villages and cities. Molten masses of rock thrown into the water by the upheaval of things hidden in the earth will cause the water to boil and send forth rocks and earth. There will be mighty earthquakes and great destruction of human life.—7BC 946 (1907).

Crime, Famines, Pestilence

Satan is working in the atmosphere; he is poisoning the atmosphere, and here we are dependent upon God for our lives—our present and eternal lives. And being in the position that we are, we need to be wide awake, wholly devoted, wholly converted, wholly consecrated to God. But we seem to sit as though we were paralyzed. God of heaven, wake us up!—2SM 52 (1890).

God has not restrained the powers of darkness from carrying forward their deadly work of vitiating the air, one of the sources of life and nutrition, with a deadly miasma. Not only is vegetable life affected but man suffers from pestilence. . . . These things are the result of drops from the vials of God's wrath[3] being sprinkled on the earth, and are but faint representations of what will be in the near future.—3SM 391 (1891).

Famines will increase. Pestilences will sweep away thousands. Dangers are all around us from the powers without and satanic workings within, but the restraining power of God is now being exercised. —19MR 382 (1897).

I have been shown that the Spirit of the Lord is being withdrawn from the earth. God's keeping power will soon be refused to all who continue to disregard His commandments. The reports of fraudulent transactions, murders, and crimes of every kind are coming to us daily. Iniquity is becoming so common a thing that it no longer shocks the senses as it once did. —Letter 258, 1907.

God's Purpose in Calamities

What mean the awful calamities by sea—vessels hurled into eternity without a moment's warning?

---

3. God takes responsibility for that which He allows or does not prevent. See Exodus 7:3; 8:32; 1 Chronicles 10:4, 13, 14.

What mean the accidents by land—fire consuming the riches that men have hoarded, much of which has been accumulated by oppression of the poor? The Lord will not interfere to protect the property of those who transgress His law, break His covenant, and trample upon His Sabbath, accepting in its place a spurious rest day.

The plagues of God are already falling upon the earth, sweeping away the most costly structures as if by a breath of fire from heaven. Will not these judgments bring professing Christians to their senses? God permits them to come that the world may take heed, that sinners may be afraid and tremble before Him.—3MR 311 (1902).

God has a purpose in permitting these calamities to occur. They are one of His means of calling men and women to their senses. By unusual workings through nature God will express to doubting human agencies that which He clearly reveals in His Word.—19MR 279 (1902).

How frequently we hear of earthquakes and tornadoes, of destruction by fire and flood, with great loss of life and property! Apparently these calamities are capricious outbreaks of disorganized, unregulated forces of nature, wholly beyond the control of man, but in them all God's purpose may be read. They are among the agencies by which He seeks to arouse men and women to a sense of their danger.—PK 277 (c. 1914).

Coming Events Are in the Hands of the Lord

The world is not without a ruler. The program of coming events is in the hands of the Lord. The Majesty of heaven has the destiny of nations as well as the concerns of His church in His own charge.—5T 753 (1889).

These symbolical representations [the fiery serpents in the wilderness] serve a double purpose. From them God's people learn not only that the physical forces of the earth are under the control of the Creator, but also that under His control are the religious movements of the nations. Especially is this true with reference to the enforcement of Sunday observance. —19MR 281 (1902).

In the great closing work we shall meet with perplexities that we know not how to deal with, but let us not forget that the three great Powers of heaven are working, that a divine hand is on the wheel, and that God will bring His purposes to pass.—Ev 65 (1902).

As the wheel-like complications were under the guidance of the hand beneath the wings of the cherubim, so the complicated play of human events is under divine control. Amidst the strife and tumult of nations, He that sitteth above the cherubim still guides the affairs of the earth.[4]—Ed 178 (1903).

In the annals of human history, the growth of nations, the rise and fall of empires, appear as if

---

4. See Ezekiel 1:4, 26; 10:8; Daniel 4:17, 25, 32.

dependent on the will and prowess of man; the shaping of events seems, to a great degree, to be determined by his power, ambition, or caprice. But in the Word of God the curtain is drawn aside, and we behold, above, behind, and through all the play and counterplay of human interest and power and passions, the agencies of the All-merciful One, silently, patiently working out the counsels of His own will. —PK 499, 500 (c. 1914).

Heaven's Regard for Earth's Affairs

In sparing the life of the first murderer, God presented before the whole universe a lesson bearing upon the great controversy.... It was His purpose, not merely to put down the rebellion, but to demonstrate to all the universe the nature of rebellion.... The holy inhabitants of other worlds were watching with the deepest interest the events taking place on the earth....

God carries with Him the sympathy and approval of the whole universe as step by step His great plan advances to its complete fulfillment.—PP 78, 79 (1890).

The act of Christ in dying for the salvation of man would not only make heaven accessible to men, but before all the universe it would justify God and His son in their dealing with the rebellion of Satan.—PP 68, 69 (1890).

The whole universe is watching with inexpressible interest the closing scenes of the great controversy between good and evil.—PK 148 (c. 1914).

Our little world is the lesson book of the universe.
—DA 19 (1898).[5]

---

5. Ellen White states that the unfallen worlds and the heavenly angels watched Christ's struggle in Gethsemane "with intense interest" (DA 693). In discussing Christ's four-thousand-year battle with Satan and His ultimate victory on the cross she uses such phrases as "the heavenly universe beheld," "all heaven and the unfallen worlds had been witnesses," "they heard," "they saw," "heaven viewed," "what a sight for the heavenly universe!" See *The Desire of Ages*, pp. 693, 759, 760.

3.

"When Shall These Things Be?"

The Disciples Ask Christ About His Return

Christ's words [Matt. 24:2] had been spoken in the hearing of a large number of people, but when He was alone, Peter, John, James, and Andrew came to Him as He sat upon the Mount of Olives. "Tell us," they said, "when shall these things be? and what shall be the sign of Thy coming, and of the end of the world?"

Jesus did not answer His disciples by taking up separately the destruction of Jerusalem and the great day of His coming. He mingled the description of these two events. Had He opened to His disciples future events as He beheld them, they would have been unable to endure the sight. In mercy to them He blended the description of the two great crises, leaving the disciples to study out the meaning for themselves.—DA 628 (1898).

Time of Christ's Return Not Known

Many who have called themselves Adventists have been time-setters. Time after time has been set for

Christ to come, but repeated failures have been the result. The definite time of our Lord's coming is declared to be beyond the ken of mortals. Even the angels, who minister unto those who shall be heirs of salvation, know not the day nor the hour. "But of that day and hour knoweth no man, no, not the angels of heaven, but My Father only." —4T 307 (1879).

We are not to know the definite time either for the outpouring of the Holy Spirit or for the coming of Christ. . . . Why has not God given us this knowledge?—Because we would not make a right use of it if He did. A condition of things would result from this knowledge among our people that would greatly retard the work of God in preparing a people to stand in the great day that is to come. We are not to live upon time excitement. . . .

You will not be able to say that He will come in one, two, or five years, neither are you to put off His coming by stating that it may not be for ten or twenty years.—RH March 22, 1892.

We are nearing the great day of God. The signs are fulfilling. And yet we have no message to tell us of the day and hour of Christ's appearing. The Lord has wisely concealed this from us that we may always be in a state of expectancy and preparation for the second appearing of our Lord Jesus Christ in the clouds of heaven.—Letter 28, 1897.

The exact time of the second coming of the Son of man is God's mystery.—DA 633 (1898).

Ours Is Not a Time-setting Message

We are not of that class who define the exact period of time that shall elapse before the coming of Jesus the second time with power and great glory. Some have set a time, and when that has passed, their presumptuous spirits have not accepted rebuke, but they have set another and another time. But many successive failures have stamped them as false prophets.—FE 335 (1895).

God gives no man a message that it will be five years or ten years or twenty years before this earth's history shall close. He would not give any living being an excuse for delaying the preparation for His appearing. He would have no one say, as did the unfaithful servant, "My lord delayeth his coming," for this leads to reckless neglect of the opportunities and privileges given to prepare us for that great day.—RH Nov. 27, 1900.

Time-setting Leads to Unbelief

Because the times repeatedly set have passed, the world is in a more decided state of unbelief than before in regard to the near advent of Christ. They look upon the failures of the time-setters with disgust, and because men have been so deceived, they turn from the truth substantiated by the Word of God that the end of all things is *at hand*.—4T 307 (1879).

I understand that Brother [E. P.] Daniels has, as it were, set time, stating that the Lord will come within five years. Now I hope the impression will not go abroad that we are time-setters. Let no such remarks be made. They do no good. Seek not to obtain a revival upon any such grounds, but let due caution be used in every word uttered, that fanatical ones will not seize anything they can get to create an excitement and the Spirit of the Lord be grieved.

We want not to move the people's passions to get up a stir, where feelings are moved and principle does not control. I feel that we need to be guarded on every side, because Satan is at work to do his uttermost to insinuate his arts and devices that shall be a power to do harm. Anything that will make a stir, create an excitement on a wrong basis, is to be dreaded, for the reaction will surely come.—Letter 34, 1887.

There will always be false and fanatical movements made by persons in the church who claim to be led of God—those who will run before they are sent and will give day and date for the occurrence of unfulfilled prophecy. The enemy is pleased to have them do this, for their successive failures and leading into false lines cause confusion and unbelief.—2SM 84 (1897).

No Time Prophecy Beyond 1844

I plainly stated at the Jackson camp meeting to these fanatical parties that they were doing the work of the adversary of souls; they were in darkness. They claimed to have great light that probation would close in October, 1884. I there stated in public that the Lord had been pleased to show me that there would be no definite time in the message given of God since 1844. —2SM 73 (1885).

Our position has been one of waiting and watching, with no time-proclamation to intervene between the close of the prophetic periods in 1844 and the time of our Lord's coming.—10MR 270 (1888).

The people will not have another message upon definite time. After this period of time [Rev. 10:4-6], reaching from 1842 to 1844, there can be no definite tracing of the prophetic time. The longest reckoning reaches to the autumn of 1844.—7BC 971 (1900).

Ellen White Expected
Christ's Return in Her Day

I was shown the company present at the Conference. Said the angel: "Some food for worms, some subjects of the seven last plagues, some will be alive and remain upon the earth to be translated at the coming of Jesus."—1T 131, 132 (1856).

Because time is short, we should work with diligence and double energy. Our children may never enter college.—3T 159 (1872).

It is really not wise to have children now. Time is short, the perils of the last days are upon us, and the little children will be largely swept off before this. —Letter 48, 1876.

In this age of the world, as the scenes of earth's history are soon to close and we are about to enter upon the time of trouble such as never was, the fewer the marriages contracted the better for all, both men and women.—5T 366 (1885).

The hour will come; it is not far distant, and some of us who now believe will be alive upon the earth, and shall see the prediction verified, and hear the voice of the archangel and the trump of God echo from mountain and plain and sea to the uttermost parts of the earth.—RH July 31, 1888.

The time of test is just upon us, for the loud cry of the third angel has already begun in the revelation of the righteousness of Christ, the sin-pardoning Redeemer.—1SM 363 (1892).

The Delay Explained

The long night of gloom is trying, but the morning is deferred in mercy, because if the Master should come so many would be found unready.—2T 194 (1868).

Had Adventists after the great disappointment in 1844 held fast their faith and followed on unitedly in the opening providence of God, receiving the message of the third angel and in the power of the Holy Spirit proclaiming it to the world, they would have seen the salvation of God, the Lord would have wrought mightily with their efforts, the work would have been completed, and Christ would have come ere this to receive His people to their reward. . . . It was not the will of God that the coming of Christ should be thus delayed. . . .

For forty years did unbelief, murmuring, and rebellion shut out ancient Israel from the land of Canaan. The same sins have delayed the entrance of modern Israel into the heavenly Canaan. In neither case were the promises of God at fault. It is the unbelief, the worldliness, unconsecration, and strife among the Lord's professed people that have kept us in this world of sin and sorrow so many years. —Ev 695, 696 (1883).

Had the church of Christ done her appointed work as the Lord ordained, the whole world would before this have been warned and the Lord Jesus would have come to our earth in power and great glory.—DA 633, 634 (1898).

God's Promises Are Conditional

The angels of God in their messages to men represent time as very short.[1] Thus it has always been presented to me. It is true that time has continued longer than we expected in the early days of this message. Our Saviour did not appear as soon as we hoped. But has the Word of the Lord failed? Never! It should be remembered that the promises and threatenings of God are alike conditional.[2] . . .

---

1. See Romans 13:11, 12; 1 Corinthians 7:29; 1 Thessalonians 4:15, 17; Hebrews 10:25; James 5:8, 9; 1 Peter 4:7; Revelation 22:6, 7.
2. See Jeremiah 18:7-10; Jonah 3:4-10.

We may have to remain here in this world because of insubordination many more years, as did the children of Israel, but for Christ's sake His people should not add sin to sin by charging God with the consequence of their own wrong course of action.—Ev 695, 696 (1901).

What Christ Is Waiting For

Christ is waiting with longing desire for the manifestation of Himself in His church. When the character of Christ shall be perfectly reproduced in His people, then He will come to claim them as His own.

It is the privilege of every Christian, not only to look for, but to hasten the coming of our Lord Jesus Christ. Were all who profess His name bearing fruit to His glory, how quickly the whole world would be sown with the seed of the gospel. Quickly the last great harvest would be ripened, and Christ would come to gather the precious grain.—COL 69 (1900).

By giving the gospel to the world it is in our power to hasten our Lord's return. We are not only to look for but to hasten the coming of the day of God (2 Pet. 3:12, margin).—DA 633 (1898).

He has put it in our power, through cooperation with Him, to bring this scene of misery to an end.—Ed 264 (1903).

A Limit to God's Forbearance

With unerring accuracy the Infinite One still keeps an account with all nations. While His mercy is tendered with calls to repentance this account will remain open, but when the figures reach a certain amount, which God has fixed, the ministry of His wrath commences.—5T 208 (1882).

God keeps a record with the nations. The figures are swelling against them in the books of heaven, and when it shall have become a law that the transgression of the first day of the week shall be met with punishment, then their cup will be full.—7BC 910 (1886).

God keeps a reckoning with the nations. . . . When the time fully comes that iniquity shall have reached the stated boundary of God's mercy, His forbearance will cease. When the accumulated figures in heaven's record books shall mark the sum of transgression complete, wrath will come.—5T 524 (1889).

While God's mercy bears long with the transgressor, there is a limit beyond which men may not go on in sin. When that limit is reached, then the offers of mercy are withdrawn, and the ministration of judgment begins.—PP 162, 165 (1890).

The time is coming when in their fraud and insolence men will reach a point that the Lord will not permit them to pass and they will learn that there is a limit to the forbearance of Jehovah.—9T 13 (1909).

There is a limit beyond which the judgments of Jehovah can no longer be delayed.—PK 417 (c. 1914).

Transgression Has Almost Reached Its Limit

Time will last a little longer until the inhabitants of the earth have filled up the cup of their iniquity, and then the wrath of God, which has so long slumbered, will awake, and this land of light will drink the cup of His unmingled wrath.—1T 363 (1863).

The cup of iniquity is nearly filled, and the retributive justice of God is about to descend upon the guilty.—4T 489 (1880).

The wickedness of the inhabitants of the world has almost filled up the measure of their iniquity. This earth has almost reached the place where God will permit the destroyer to work his will upon it.—7T 141 (1902).

Transgression has almost reached its limit. Confusion fills the world, and a great terror is soon to come upon human beings. The end is very near. We who know the truth should be preparing for what is soon to break upon the world as an overwhelming surprise.—8T 28 (1904).

We Should Keep the Great Day of God Before Our Minds

We must educate ourselves to be thinking and dwelling upon the great scenes of the judgment just before us and then, as we keep the scenes of the great day of God before us when everything will be revealed, it will have an effect upon our character. One brother said to me, "Sister White, do you think the Lord will come in ten

years?" "What difference does it make to you whether
He shall come in two, four, or ten years?" "Why," said
he, "I think I would do differently in some things than
I now do if I knew the Lord was to come in ten years."

"What would you do?" said I.

"Why," said he, "I would sell my property and begin
to search the Word of God and try to warn the people
and get them to prepare for His coming, and I would
plead with God that I might be ready to meet Him."

Then said I, "If you knew that the Lord was not
coming for twenty years, you would live differently?"

Said he, "I think I would." . . .

How selfish was the expression that he would live
a different life if he knew his Lord was to come in ten
years! Why, Enoch walked with God 300 years. This
is a lesson for us that we shall walk with God every
day, and we are not safe unless we are waiting and
watching.—Ms 10, 1886.

The Shortness of Time

May the Lord give no rest, day nor night, to those
who are now careless and indolent in the cause and
work of God. The end is near. This is that which Jesus
would have us keep ever before us—the shortness of
time.—Letter 97, 1886.

When we shall stand with the redeemed upon the
sea of glass with harps of gold and crowns of glory and
before us the unmeasured eternity, we shall then see
how short was the waiting period of probation.
—10MR 266 (1886).

4.
God's Last Day Church[1]

God's People Keep His Commandments

God has a church on earth who are lifting up the downtrodden law, and presenting to the world the Lamb of God that taketh away the sins of the world. . . .

There is but one church in the world who are at the present time standing in the breach and making up the hedge, building up the old waste places. . . .

Let all be careful not to make an outcry against the only people who are fulfilling the description given of the remnant people, who keep the commandments of God and have faith in Jesus. . . . God has a distinct people, a church on earth, second to none, but superior to all in their facilities to teach the truth, to vindicate the law of God. . . . My brother, if you are teaching that the Seventh-day Adventist Church is Babylon, you are wrong.—TM 50, 58, 59 (1893).

---

1. The book of Revelation focuses on two sets of God's people—the visible remnant (12:17) and "My people" in Babylon (18:4). This chapter deals with the former, and chapter 14, "The Loud Cry," deals with the latter.

They Have the Testimony of Jesus

As the end draws near and the work of giving the
last warning to the world extends, it becomes more
important for those who accept present truth to have
a clear understanding of the nature and influence of
the testimonies, which God in His providence has
linked with the work of the third angel's message from
its very rise.—5T 654 (1889).

Men may get up scheme after scheme and the
enemy will seek to seduce souls from the truth, but all
who believe that the Lord has spoken through Sister
White and has given her a message will be safe from
the many delusions that will come in these last days.
—3SM 83, 84 (1906).

There will be those who will claim to have visions.
When God gives you clear evidence that the vision is
from Him, you may accept it, but do not accept it on
any other evidence, for people are going to be led more
and more astray in foreign countries and in America.
—2SM 72 (1905).

Their "Landmark" Biblical Doctrines

The passing of the time in 1844 was a period of great
events, opening to our astonished eyes the cleansing
of the sanctuary transpiring in heaven, and having
decided relation to God's people upon the earth, [also]
the first and second angels' messages and the third,
unfurling the banner on which was inscribed, "The

commandments of God and the faith of Jesus." One of the landmarks under this message was the temple of God, seen by His truth-loving people in heaven, and the ark containing the law of God. The light of the Sabbath of the fourth commandment flashed its strong rays in the pathway of the transgressors of God's law. The nonimmortality of the wicked is an old landmark. I can call to mind nothing more that can come under the head of the old landmarks.—CW 30, 31 (1889).

The Distinctive Mission
of Seventh-day Adventists

The Lord has made us the depositaries of His law; He has committed to us sacred and eternal truth, which is to be given to others in faithful warnings, reproofs, and encouragement.—5T 381 (1885).

Seventh-day Adventists have been chosen by God as a peculiar people, separate from the world. By the great cleaver of truth He has cut them out from the quarry of the world and brought them into connection with Himself. He has made them His representatives and has called them to be ambassadors for Him in the last work of salvation. The greatest wealth of truth ever entrusted to mortals, the most solemn and fearful warnings ever sent by God to man, have been committed to them to be given to the world.—7T 138 (1902).

In a special sense Seventh-day Adventists have been set in the world as watchmen and light bearers. To them has been entrusted the last warning for a perishing world. On them is shining wonderful light from the Word of God. They have been given a work of the most solemn import—the proclamation of the first, second, and third angels' messages. There is no other work of so great importance. They are to allow nothing else to absorb their attention.—9T 19 (1909).

Reasons Why the Seventh-day Adventist Church Was Organized

As our numbers increased it was evident that without some form of organization there would be great confusion, and the work would not be carried forward successfully. To provide for the support of the ministry, for carrying the work in new fields, for protecting both the churches and the ministry from unworthy members, for holding church property, for the publication of the truth through the press, and for many other objects, organization was indispensable. . . .

Light was given by His Spirit that there must be order and thorough discipline in the church—that organization was essential. System and order are manifest in all the works of God throughout the universe. Order is the law of heaven, and it should be the law of God's people on the earth.—TM 26 (1902).

Organization Will Always Be Essential

Unless the churches are so organized that they can carry out and enforce order, they have nothing to hope for in the future.—1T 270 (1862).

Oh, how Satan would rejoice if he could succeed in his efforts to get in among this people and disorganize the work at a time when thorough organization is essential and will be the greatest power to keep out spurious uprisings and to refute claims not endorsed by the Word of God! We want to hold the lines evenly, that there shall be no breaking down of the system of organization and order that has been built up by wise, careful labor. License must not be given to disorderly elements that desire to control the work at this time.

Some have advanced the thought that, as we near the close of time, every child of God will act independently of any religious organization. But I have been instructed by the Lord that in this work there is no such thing as every man's being independent.[2] —9T 257, 258 (1909).

As we near the final crisis, instead of feeling that there is less need of order and harmony of action, we should be more systematic than heretofore.—3SM 26 (1892).

The Special Authority of God's Church

God has invested His church with special authority and power which no one can be justified in disregarding and despising, for in so doing he despises the voice of God.—3T 417 (1875).

God has bestowed the highest power under heaven upon His church. It is the voice of God in His united

2. From manuscript read before the delegates at the General Conference Session, Washington, D.C., May 30, 1909.

people in church capacity which is to be respected.
—3T 451 (1875).

A Time of Spiritual Weakness and Blindness

I was confirmed in all I had stated in Minneapolis,
that a reformation must go through the churches.
Reforms must be made, for spiritual weakness and
blindness were upon the people who had been blessed
with great light and precious opportunities and privileges. As reformers they had come out of the denomi-
national churches, but they now act a part similar to
that which the churches acted. We hoped that there
would not be the necessity for another coming out.[3]
While we will endeavor to keep the "unity of the
Spirit" in the bonds of peace, we will not with pen or
voice cease to protest against bigotry.—EGW'88 356,
357 (1889).

Of those who boast of their light and yet fail to walk
in it Christ says, "But I say unto you, It shall be more
tolerable for Tyre and Sidon at the day of judgment
than for you. And thou, Capernaum [Seventh-day Adventists, who have had great light], which art exalted
unto heaven [in point of privilege], shalt be brought
down to hell: for if the mighty works which have been
done in thee had been done in Sodom, it would have
remained until this day."—RH Aug. 1, 1893.[4]

---

3. This is the only known statement from the pen of Ellen White
indicating that she might have lost confidence in the Seventh-day
Adventist church organization. The doubt which she expressed here
was never repeated during the remaining twenty-six years of her life.
4. The bracketed comments are by Ellen White.

The church is in the Laodicean state. The presence of God is not in her midst.—1NL 99 (1898).

Abuse of Power at Church Headquarters

The General Conference is itself becoming corrupted with wrong sentiments and principles. . . .

Men have taken unfair advantage of those whom they supposed to be under their jurisdiction. They were determined to bring the individuals to their terms; they would rule or ruin. . . .

The high-handed power that has been developed, as though position has made men gods, makes me afraid, and ought to cause fear. It is a curse wherever and by whomsoever it is exercised.—TM 359-361 (1895).

There are altogether too many weighty responsibilities given to a few men, and some do not make God their Counselor. What do these men know of the necessities of the work in foreign countries? How can they know how to decide the questions which come to them asking for information? It would require three months for those in foreign countries to receive a response to their questions, even if there was no delay in writing.—TM 321 (1896).

Those living in distant countries will not do that which their judgment tells them is right unless they first send for permission to Battle Creek. Before they will advance they await Yes or No from that place. —SpT-A(9) 32 (1896).

It is not wise to choose one man as president of the General Conference. The work of the General Conference has extended, and some things have been made unnecessarily complicated. A want of discernment has been shown. There should be a division of the field, or some other plan should be devised to change the present order of things.[5]—TM 342 (1896).

Unwise Leaders Do Not Speak for God

The voice from Battle Creek, which has been regarded as authority in counseling how the work should be done, is no longer the voice of God.—17MR 185 (1896).

It has been some years since I have considered the General Conference as the voice of God.—17MR 216 (1898).

That these men should stand in a sacred place, to be as the voice of God to the people, as we once believed

---

5. The Seventh-day Adventist Church was organized in 1863 with 3,500 members, half a dozen local conferences, about thirty ministerial laborers, and a General Conference committee of three. The General Conference president was well able to provide the leadership and counsel required by such a small organization. He could personally attend every important meeting and in addition give personal attention to much of the business connected with the publishing work. However, by 1896 the work of the church had greatly expanded in the United States, and extended to Europe, Australia, and Africa as well. It was no longer possible for one man to give adequate supervision and direction to such a widespreading work. Ellen White urged a division of the field, so that our church members around the world would not look to just one man for counsel. This was accomplished by the creation of union conferences and world divisions.

the General Conference to be—that is past.—GCB
April 3, 1901, p. 25.

A New Denomination Not Needed

You will take passages in the *Testimonies* that
speak of the close of probation, of the shaking among
God's people, and you will talk of a coming out from
this people of a purer, holier people that will arise.
Now all this pleases the enemy. . . . Should many
accept the views you advance, and talk and act upon
them, we would see one of the greatest fanatical
excitements that has ever been witnessed among
Seventh-day Adventists. This is what Satan wants.
—1SM 179 (1890).

The Lord has not given you a message to call the
Seventh-day Adventists Babylon, and to call the people
of God to come out of her. All the reasons you may
present cannot have weight with me on this subject,
because the Lord has given me decided light that is
opposed to such a message. . . .

I know that the Lord loves His church. It is not to
be disorganized or broken up into independent atoms.
There is not the least consistency in this; there is not
the least evidence that such a thing will be.—2SM 63,
68, 69 (1893).

I tell you, my brethren, the Lord has an organized
body through whom He will work. . . . When anyone
is drawing apart from the organized body of God's
commandment-keeping people, when he begins to
weigh the church in his human scales and begins to

pronounce judgment against them, then you may know that God is not leading him. He is on the wrong track.—3SM 17, 18 (1893).

God Will Set Everything in Order

There is no need to doubt, to be fearful that the work will not succeed. God is at the head of the work, and He will set everything in order. If matters need adjusting at the head of the work God will attend to that, and work to right every wrong. Let us have faith that God is going to carry the noble ship which bears the people of God safely into port.—2SM 390 (1892).

Has God no living church? He has a church, but it is the church militant, not the church triumphant. We are sorry that there are defective members, that there are tares amid the wheat. . . . Although there are evils existing in the church, and will be until the end of the world, the church in these last days is to be the light of the world that is polluted and demoralized by sin. The church, enfeebled and defective, needing to be reproved, warned, and counseled, is the only object upon earth upon which Christ bestows His supreme regard.—TM 45, 49 (1893).

The bulwarks of Satan will never triumph. Victory will attend the third angel's message. As the Captain of the Lord's host tore down the walls of Jericho, so will the Lord's commandment-keeping people triumph, and all opposing elements be defeated.—TM 410 (1898).

Distribution of Responsibility Urged

What we want now is a reorganization. We want to begin at the foundation, and to build upon a different principle. . . .

Here are men who are standing at the head of our various institutions, of the educational interests, and of the conferences in different localities and in different States. All these are to stand as representative men, to have a voice in molding and fashioning the plans that shall be carried out. There are to be more than one or two or three men to consider the whole vast field. The work is great, and there is no one human mind that can plan for the work which needs to be done. . . .

Now I want to say, God has not put any kingly power in our ranks to control this or that branch of the work. The work has been greatly restricted by the efforts to control it in every line. . . . There must be a renovation, a reorganization; a power and strength must be brought into the committees that are necessary."[6]—GCB April 3, 1901, pp. 25, 26.

New Conferences must be formed. It was in the order of God that the Union conference was organized in Australasia. . . . It is not necessary to send thousands of miles to Battle Creek for advice, and then have to wait weeks for an answer. Those who are right on the ground are to decide what shall be done.—GCB April 5, 1901, pp. 69, 70.

---

6. From Ellen White's opening address on April 2, 1901, to the General Conference Session in Battle Creek.

The 1901 General
Conference Session Responds

Who do you suppose has been among us since this Conference began? Who has kept away the objectionable features that generally appear in such a meeting? Who has walked up and down the aisles of this Tabernacle? The God of heaven and His angels. And they did not come here to tear you in pieces, but to give you right and peaceable minds. They have been among us to work the works of God, to keep back the powers of darkness, that the work God designed should be done should not be hindered. The angels of God have been working among us. . . .

I was never more astonished in my life than at the turn things have taken at this meeting. This is not our work. God has brought it about. Instruction regarding this was presented to me, but until the sum was worked out at this meeting I could not comprehend this instruction. God's angels have been walking up and down in this congregation. I want every one of you to remember this, and I want you to remember also that God has said that He will heal the wounds of His people.—GCB April 25, 1901, pp. 463, 464.

During the General Conference the Lord wrought mightily for His people. Every time I think of that meeting, a sweet solemnity comes over me, and sends a glow of gratitude to my soul. We have seen the stately steppings of the Lord our Redeemer. We praise His holy name, for He has brought deliverance to His people.—RH Nov. 26, 1901.

It has been a necessity to organize union conferences, that the General Conference shall not exercise dictation over all the separate conferences. The power vested in the Conference is not to be centered in one man, or two men, or six men; there is to be a council of men over the separate divisions.[7]—Ms 26, April 3, 1903.

Confidence in SDA Organization Reaffirmed

We cannot now step off the foundation that God has established. We cannot now enter into any new organization, for this would mean apostasy from the truth.—2SM 390 (1905).

I am instructed to say to Seventh-day Adventists the world over, God has called us as a people to be a peculiar treasure unto Himself. He has appointed that His church on earth shall stand perfectly united in the Spirit and counsel of the Lord of hosts to the end of time.—2SM 397 (1908).

At times, when a small group of men entrusted with the general management of the work have, in the name of the General Conference, sought to carry out unwise plans to restrict God's work, I have said that I could no longer regard the voice of the General Conference, represented by these few men, as the voice of God. But this is not saying that the decisions

7. For further information regarding organizational changes made at the 1901 General Conference Session see the *Seventh-day Adventist Encyclopedia* (vol. 10 of the Commentary Reference Series), revised edition, pp. 1050-1053.

of a General Conference composed of an assembly of duly appointed, representative men from all parts of the field should not be respected.

God has ordained that the representatives of His church from all parts of the earth, when assembled in a General Conference, shall have authority. The error that some are in danger of committing is in giving to the mind and judgment of one man, or of a small group of men, the full measure of authority and influence that God has invested in His church in the judgment and voice of the General Conference assembled to plan for the prosperity and advancement of His work. —9T 260, 261 (1909).

God has invested His church with special authority and power which no one can be justified in disregarding and despising, for he who does this despises the voice of God.—AA 164 (1911).

I am encouraged and blessed as I realize that the God of Israel is still guiding His people and that He will continue to be with them, even to the end.[8]—2SM 406 (1913).

A Statement by W. C. White

I told her [Mrs. Lida Scott] how Mother regarded the experience of the remnant church, and of her positive

---

8. From Ellen White's final message to the Seventh-day Adventist Church in General Conference Session. These reassuring words were read to the session by the General Conference president, A. G. Daniells, on May 27, 1913.

teaching that God would not permit this denomination to so fully apostatize that there would be the coming out of another church.—W. C. White to E. E. Andross, May 23, 1915, White Estate Correspondence File.

Spiritual Revival Still Needed

One day at noon I was writing of the work that might have been done at the last [1901] General Conference if the men in positions of trust had followed the will and way of God. Those who have had great light have not walked in the light. The meeting was closed, and the break was not made. Men did not humble themselves before the Lord as they should have done, and the Holy Spirit was not imparted.

I had written thus far when I lost consciousness, and I seemed to be witnessing a scene in Battle Creek.

We were assembled in the auditorium of the Tabernacle. Prayer was offered, a hymn was sung, and prayer was again offered. Most earnest supplication was made to God. The meeting was marked by the presence of the Holy Spirit. . . .

No one seemed to be too proud to make heartfelt confession, and those who led in this work were the ones who had influence, but had not before had courage to confess their sins.

There was rejoicing such as never before had been heard in the Tabernacle.

Then I aroused from my unconsciousness, and for a while could not think where I was. My pen was still in my hand. The words were spoken to me: *"This *might have been*. All this the Lord was waiting to do for His people. All heaven was waiting to be gracious." I thought of where we might have been had thorough work been done at the last General Conference. —8T 104-106 (Jan. 5, 1903).

I have been deeply impressed by scenes that have recently passed before me in the night season. There seemed to be a great movement—a work of revival— going forward in many places. Our people were moving into line, responding to God's call.[9]—TM 515 (1913).

The Patience of God With His People

The church has failed, sadly failed, to meet the expectations of her Redeemer, and yet the Lord does not withdraw Himself from His people. He bears with them still, not because of any goodness found in them, but that His name may not be dishonored before the enemies of truth and righteousness, that the satanic agencies may not triumph in the destruction of God's people. He has borne long with their waywardness, unbelief and folly. With wonderful forbearance and compassion He has disciplined them. If they will heed His instruction He will cleanse away their perverse tendencies, saving them with an everlasting salvation and making them eternal monuments of the power of His grace.—ST Nov. 13, 1901.

We should remember that the church, enfeebled and defective though it be, is the only object on earth

9. From Ellen White's first message to the General Conference Session of 1913.

on which Christ bestows His supreme regard. He is constantly watching it with solicitude, and is strengthening it by His Holy Spirit.—2SM 396 (1902).

God Works With Those
Who Are Faithful to Him

The Lord Jesus will always have a chosen people to serve Him. When the Jewish people rejected Christ, the Prince of life, He took from them the kingdom of God and gave it unto the Gentiles. God will continue to work on this principle with every branch of His work.

When a church proves unfaithful to the word of the Lord, whatever their position may be, however high and sacred their calling, the Lord can no longer work with them. Others are then chosen to bear important responsibilities. But, if these in turn do not purify their lives from every wrong action, if they do not establish pure and holy principles in all their borders, then the Lord will grievously afflict and humble them and, unless they repent, will remove them from their place and make them a reproach.—14MR 102 (1903).

Judged by the Light Bestowed

In the balances of the sanctuary the Seventh-day Adventist church is to be weighed. She will be judged by the privileges and advantages that she has had. If her spiritual experience does not correspond to the advantages that Christ, at infinite cost, has bestowed on her, if the blessings conferred have not qualified her to do the work entrusted to her, on her will be pronounced the sentence: "Found wanting." By the light bestowed, the opportunities given, will she be judged. . . .

Solemn admonitions of warning, manifest in the destruction of dearly cherished facilities[10] for service, say to us: "Remember therefore from whence thou art fallen, and repent, and do the first works" (Rev. 2:5). . . .

Unless the church, which is now being leavened with her own backsliding, shall repent and be converted, she will eat of the fruit of her own doing, until she shall abhor herself. When she resists the evil and chooses the good, when she seeks God with all humility and reaches her high calling in Christ, standing on the platform of eternal truth and by faith laying hold upon the attainments prepared for her, she will be healed. She will appear in her God-given simplicity and purity, separate from earthly entanglements, showing that the truth has made her free indeed. Then her members will indeed be the chosen of God, His representatives.—8T 247-251 (April 21, 1903).

Israel's History a Warning to Us

In these last days God's people will be exposed to the very same dangers as were ancient Israel. Those who will not receive the warnings that God gives will fall into the same perils as did ancient Israel and come short of entering into rest through unbelief. Ancient Israel suffered calamities on account of their

---

10. The Battle Creek Sanitarium, the largest and best-known Adventist institution in the world, burned to the ground February 18, 1902. This was followed by the destruction of the Review and Herald Publishing Association, also by fire, on December 30, 1902.

unsanctified hearts and unsubmitted wills. Their final rejection as a nation was a result of their own unbelief, self-confidence, impenitence, blindness of mind, and hardness of heart. In their history we have a danger signal lifted before us.

"Take heed, brethren, lest there be in any of you an evil heart of unbelief, in departing from the living God. . . . For we are made partakers of Christ, if we hold the beginning of our confidence stedfast unto the end" (Heb. 3:12, 14).—Letter 30, 1895.

The Church Militant Is Imperfect

The church militant is not the church triumphant, and earth is not heaven. The church is composed of erring, imperfect men and women, who are but learners in the school of Christ, to be trained, disciplined, educated, for this life and for the future, immortal life.—ST Jan. 4, 1883.

Some people seem to think that upon entering the church they will have their expectations fulfilled, and meet only with those who are pure and perfect. They are zealous in their faith, and when they see faults in church members, they say, "We left the world in order to have no association with evil characters, but the evil is here also;" and they ask, as did the servants in the parable, "From whence then hath it tares?" But we need not be thus disappointed, for the Lord has not warranted us in coming to the conclusion that the church is perfect; and all our zeal will not be successful

in making the church militant as pure as the church
triumphant.—TM 47 (1893).

The Church Triumphant
Will Be Faithful and Christlike

The work is soon to close. The members of the
church militant who have proved faithful will become
the church triumphant.—Ev 707 (1892).

The life of Christ was a life charged with a divine
message of the love of God, and He longed intensely to
impart this love to others in rich measure. Compassion beamed from His countenance, and His conduct
was characterized by grace, humility, truth, and love.
Every member of His church militant must manifest
the same qualities, if he would join the church triumphant.—FE 179 (1891).

5.

Devotional Life of the Remnant

A Twofold Life

In this age, just prior to the second coming of Christ in the clouds of heaven, such a work as that of John [the Baptist] is to be done. God calls for men who will prepare a people to stand in the great day of the Lord. . . . In order to give such a message as John gave, we must have a spiritual experience like his. The same work must be wrought in us. We must behold God, and in beholding Him lose sight of self.—8T 332, 333 (1904).

Communion with God will ennoble the character and the life. Men will take knowledge of us, as of the first disciples, that we have been with Jesus. This will impart to the worker a power that nothing else can give. Of this power he must not allow himself to be deprived. We must live a twofold life—a life of thought and action, of silent prayer and earnest work.—MH 512 (1905).

Prayer and effort, effort and prayer, will be the business of your life. You must pray as though the efficiency and praise were all due to God, and labor as though duty were all your own.—4T 538 (1881).

No man is safe for a day or an hour without prayer.—GC 530 (1911).

He who does nothing but pray will soon cease to pray.—SC 101 (1892).

Firmly Rooted in Christ

The storm is coming, the storm that will try every man's faith of what sort it is. Believers must now be firmly rooted in Christ or else they will be led astray by some phase of error.—Ev 361, 362 (1905).

It would be well for us to spend a thoughtful hour each day in contemplation of the life of Christ. We should take it point by point and let the imagination grasp each scene, especially the closing ones.—DA 83 (1898).

The only defense against evil is the indwelling of Christ in the heart through faith in His righteousness. Unless we become vitally connected with God, we can never resist the unhallowed effects of self-love, self-indulgence, and temptation to sin. We may leave off many bad habits, for the time we may part company with Satan; but without a vital connection with God, through the surrender of ourselves to Him moment by moment, we shall be overcome. Without a personal acquaintance with Christ, and a continual communion, we are at the mercy of the enemy, and shall do his bidding in the end.—DA 324 (1898).

Christ and Him crucified should be the theme of contemplation, of conversation, and of our most joyful emotion.—SC 103, 104 (1892).

Molded by the Holy Spirit

Never will the human heart know happiness until it is submitted to be molded by the Spirit of God. The Spirit conforms the renewed soul to the model, Jesus Christ. Through its influence, enmity against God is changed into faith and love, and pride into humility. The soul perceives the beauty of truth, and Christ is honored in excellence and perfection of character. —OHC 152 (1896).

There is not an impulse of our nature, not a faculty of the mind or an inclination of the heart, but needs to be, moment by moment, under the control of the Spirit of God.—PP 421 (1890).

The Spirit illumines our darkness, informs our ignorance, and helps us in our manifold necessities. But the mind must be constantly going out after God. If worldliness is allowed to come in, if we have no desire to pray, no desire to commune with Him who is the source of strength and wisdom, the Spirit will not abide with us.—OHC 154 (1904).

The Necessity of Bible Study

No renewed heart can be kept in a condition of sweetness without the daily application of the salt of the Word. Divine grace must be received daily, or no man will stay converted.—OHC 215 (1897).

Let your faith be substantiated by the Word of God. Grasp firmly the living testimony of truth. Have faith in Christ as a personal Saviour. He has been and ever will be our Rock of Ages.—Ev 362 (1905).

Christians should be preparing for what is soon to break upon the world as an overwhelming surprise, and this preparation they should make by diligently studying the Word of God and striving to conform their lives to its precepts.—PK 626 (c. 1914).

None but those who have fortified the mind with the truths of the Bible will stand through the last great conflict.—GC 593, 594 (1911).

Only those who have been diligent students of the Scriptures and who have received the love of the truth will be shielded from the powerful delusion that takes the world captive.—GC 625 (1911).

Our people need to understand the oracles of God; they need to have a systematic knowledge of the principles of revealed truth, which will fit them for what is coming upon the earth and prevent them from being carried about by every wind of doctrine.—5T 273 (1885).

Commit Scripture to Memory

Several times each day precious, golden moments

should be consecrated to prayer and the study of the Scriptures, if it is only to commit a text to memory, that spiritual life may exist in the soul.—4T 459 (1880).

God's precious Word is the standard for youth who would be loyal to the King of heaven. Let them study the Scriptures. Let them commit text after text to memory and acquire a knowledge of what the Lord has said.—ML 315 (1887).

Build a wall of scriptures around you, and you will see that the world cannot break it down. Commit the Scriptures to memory, and then throw right back upon Satan when he comes with his temptations, "It is written." This is the way that our Lord met the temptations of Satan, and resisted them.—RH April 10, 1888.

Hang in memory's hall the precious words of Christ. They are to be valued far above silver or gold.—6T 81 (1900).

Keep a pocket Bible with you as you work, and improve every opportunity to commit to memory its precious promises.—RH April 27, 1905.

The time will come when many will be deprived of the written Word. But if this Word is printed in the memory, no one can take it from us.— **20MR 64** (1906).

Study the Word of God. Commit its precious promises to memory so that, when we shall be deprived of

our Bibles, we may still be in possession of the Word
of God.—10MR 298 (1909).

Revelation 14 an Anchor to God's People

In these last days it is our duty to ascertain the full
meaning of the first, second, and third angels' messages. All our transactions should be in accordance
with the Word of God. The first, second, and third
angels' messages are all united and are revealed in the
fourteenth chapter of Revelation from the sixth verse
to the close.—13MR 68 (1896).

Many who embraced the third message had not had
an experience in the two former messages. Satan
understood this, and his evil eye was upon them to
overthrow them; but the third angel was pointing
them to the most holy place, and those who had an
experience in the past messages were pointing them
the way to the heavenly sanctuary. Many saw the
perfect chain of truth in the angels' messages and
gladly received them in their order, and followed
Jesus by faith into the heavenly sanctuary. These
messages were represented to me as an anchor to the
people of God. Those who understand and receive
them will be kept from being swept away by the many
delusions of Satan.—EW 256 (1858).

Educate the Mind to Believe God's Word

Those who feel at liberty to question the Word of
God, to doubt everything where there is any chance to

be unbelieving, will find that it will require a tremendous struggle to have faith when trouble comes. It will be almost impossible to overcome the influence that binds the mind which has been educated in the line of unbelief, for by this course the soul is bound in Satan's snare and becomes powerless to break the dreadful net that has been woven closer and closer about the soul.

In taking a position of doubt, man calls to his aid the agencies of Satan. But the only hope of one who has been educated in the line of unbelief is to fall all helpless upon the Saviour and, like a child, submit his will and his way to Christ that he may be brought out of darkness into His marvelous light. Man does not have the power to recover himself from the snare of Satan. He who educates himself in the line of questioning, doubting, and criticizing strengthens himself in infidelity.—Ms 3, 1895.

Preparation for Future Trials

The servants of Christ are to prepare no set speech to present when brought to trial for their faith. Their preparation is to be made day by day, in treasuring up in their hearts the precious truths of God's Word, in feeding upon the teaching of Christ, and through prayer strengthening their faith; then, when brought into trial, the Holy Spirit will bring to their remembrance the very truths that will reach the hearts of those who shall come to hear. God will flash the knowledge obtained by diligent searching of the Scriptures into their memory at the very time when it is needed.—CSW 40, 41 (1900).

When the time of trial shall come there are men now preaching to others who will find, upon examining the positions they hold, that there are many things for which they can give no satisfactory reason. Until thus tested they knew not their great ignorance. And there are many in the church who take it for granted that they understand what they believe, but, until controversy arises, they do not know their own weakness. When separated from those of like faith and compelled to stand singly and alone to explain their belief, they will be surprised to see how confused are their ideas of what they had accepted as truth.—5T 707 (1889).

Control the Moral Powers

The ability to give a reason for our faith is a good accomplishment, but if the truth does not go deeper than this, the soul will never be saved. The heart must be purified from all moral defilement.—OHC 142 (1893).

Few realize that it is a duty to exercise control over their thoughts and imaginations. It is difficult to keep the undisciplined mind fixed upon profitable subjects. But if the thoughts are not properly employed, religion cannot flourish in the soul. The mind must be preoccupied with sacred and eternal things, or it will cherish trifling and superficial thoughts. Both the intellectual and the moral powers must be disciplined, and they will strengthen and improve by exercise.—OHC 111 (1881).

We greatly need to encourage and cultivate pure, chaste thoughts, and to strengthen the moral powers rather than the lower and carnal powers. God help us to awake from our self-indulgent appetites!—MM 278 (1896).

The Example of Enoch

Enoch walked with God three hundred years previous to his translation to heaven, and the state of the world was not then more favorable for the perfection of Christian character than it is today. And how did Enoch walk with God? He educated his mind and heart to ever feel that he was in the presence of God, and when in perplexity his prayers would ascend to God to keep him.

He refused to take any course that would offend his God. He kept the Lord continually before him. He would pray, "Teach me Thy way, that I may not err. What is Thy pleasure concerning me? What shall I do to honor Thee, my God?" Thus he was constantly shaping his way and course in accordance with God's commandments, and he had perfect confidence and trust in his heavenly Father, that He would help him. He had no thought or will of his own. It was all submerged in the will of his Father.

Now Enoch was a representative of those who will be upon the earth when Christ shall come, who will be translated to heaven without seeing death.—1SAT 32 (1886).

Enoch had temptations as well as we. He was surrounded with society no more friendly to righteousness than is that which surrounds us. The atmosphere he breathed was tainted with sin and corruption the same as ours, yet he lived a life of holiness. He was unsullied with the prevailing sins of the age in which he lived. So may we remain pure and uncorrupted.—2T 122 (1868).

Remember God's Past Blessings

In reviewing our past history, having traveled over every step of advance to our present standing, I can say, Praise God! As I see what the Lord has wrought, I am filled with astonishment, and with confidence in Christ as leader. We have nothing to fear for the future, except as we shall forget the way the Lord has led us, and His teaching in our past history.—LS 196 (1902).

A Time for Serious Reflection

If there ever was a time when serious reflection becomes every one who fears God, it is now, when personal piety is essential. The inquiry should be made, "What am I, and what is my work and mission in this time? On which side am I working—Christ's side or the enemy's side?" Let every soul now humble himself or herself before God, for now we are surely living in the great Day of Atonement. The cases even now of many are passing in review before God, for they are to sleep in their graves a little season. Your profession of faith is not your guarantee in that day, but the state of your affections. Is the soul-temple cleansed of its defilement? Are my sins confessed and am I repenting of them before God, that they may be blotted out? Do I esteem myself too lightly? Am I willing to make any and every sacrifice for the excellency of the knowledge of Jesus Christ? Do I feel every moment I am not my own, but Christ's property, that my service belongs to God, whose I am?—Ms 87, 1886.

We should ask ourselves, "For what are we living and working? And what will be the outcome of it all?"—ST Nov. 21, 1892.

Living With Reference to the Judgment Day

I have questioned in my mind, as I have seen the people in our cities hurrying to and fro with business, whether they ever thought of the day of God that is just upon us. Every one of us should be living with reference to the great day which is soon to come upon us.—1SAT 25 (1886).

We cannot afford to live with no reference to the day of judgment; for though long delayed, it is now near, even at the door, and hasteth greatly. The trumpet of the Archangel will soon startle the living and wake the dead.—CG 560, 561 (1892).

Ready for Christ's Return

If we find no pleasure now in the contemplation of heavenly things; if we have no interest in seeking the knowledge of God, no delight in beholding the character of Christ; if holiness has no attractions for us— then we may be sure that our hope of heaven is vain. Perfect conformity to the will of God is the high aim to be constantly before the Christian. He will love to talk of God, of Jesus, of the home of bliss and purity which Christ has prepared for them that love Him. The contemplation of these themes, when the soul feasts upon the blessed assurances of God, the apostle represents as tasting "the powers of the world to come." —5T 745 (1889).

If you are right with God today, you are ready if Christ should come today.—HP 227 (1891).

6.

Lifestyle and Activities of the Remnant

A Spirit of Service and Self-Sacrifice

Long has God waited for the spirit of service to take possession of the whole church so that everyone shall be working for Him according to his ability. When the members of the church of God do their appointed work in the needy fields at home and abroad, in fulfillment of the gospel commission, the whole world will soon be warned, and the Lord Jesus will return to this earth with power and great glory.—AA 111 (1911).

Everywhere there is a tendency to substitute the work of organizations for individual effort. Human wisdom tends to consolidation, to centralization, to the building up of great churches and institutions. Multitudes leave to institutions and organizations the work of benevolence; they excuse themselves from contact with the world, and their hearts grow cold. They become self-absorbed and unimpressible. Love for God and man dies out of the soul.

Christ commits to His followers an individual work—
a work that cannot be done by proxy. Ministry to the
sick and the poor, the giving of the gospel to the lost,
is not to be left to committees or organized charities.
Individual responsibility, individual effort, personal
sacrifice, is the requirement of the gospel.—MH 147
(1905).

"Occupy Till I Come"

Christ says, "Occupy till I come" [Luke 19:13]. It
may be but a few years until our life's history shall
close, but we must occupy till then.—RH April 21,
1896.

Christ would have everyone educate himself to
calmly contemplate His second appearing. All are to
search the Word of God daily, but not neglect present
duties.—Letter 28, 1897.

Christ declared that when He comes some of His
waiting people will be engaged in business transactions. Some will be sowing in the field, others reaping
and gathering in the harvest, and others grinding at
the mill. It is not God's will that His elect shall
abandon life's duties and responsibilities and give
themselves up to idle contemplation, living in a religious dream.—Ms 26, 1901.

Crowd all the good works you possibly can into this
life.—5T 488 (1889).

As If Each Day Might Be Our Last

We should watch and work and pray as though this were the last day that would be granted us.—5T 200 (1882).

Our only safety is in doing our work for each day as it comes, working, watching, waiting, every moment relying on the strength of Him who was dead and who is alive again, who lives forevermore.—Letter 66, 1894.

Each morning consecrate yourselves and your children to God for that day. Make no calculation for months or years; these are not yours. One brief day is given you. As if it were your last on earth, work during its hours for the Master. Lay all your plans before God, to be carried out or given up, as His providence shall indicate.—7T 44 (1902).

Conscientious Sabbath Observance[1]

Our heavenly Father desires through the observance of the Sabbath to preserve among men a knowledge of Himself. He desires that the Sabbath shall direct our minds to Him as the true and living God, and that through knowing Him we may have life and peace.—6T 349 (1900).

All through the week we are to have the Sabbath in mind and be making preparation to keep it according to the commandment. We are not merely to observe the

1. See "The Observance of the Sabbath," in *Testimonies for the Church*, vol. 6, pp. 349-368.

Sabbath as a legal matter. We are to understand its spiritual bearing upon all the transactions of life. . . .

When the Sabbath is thus remembered, the temporal will not be allowed to encroach upon the spiritual. No duty pertaining to the six working days will be left for the Sabbath.—6T 353, 354 (1900).

The necessities of life must be attended to, the sick must be cared for, the wants of the needy must be supplied. He will not be held guiltless who neglects to relieve suffering on the Sabbath. God's holy rest day was made for man, and acts of mercy are in perfect harmony with its intent. God does not desire His creatures to suffer an hour's pain that may be relieved upon the Sabbath or any other day.—DA 207 (1898).

Faithful in Tithes and Offerings

The tithe is sacred, reserved by God for Himself. It is to be brought into His treasury to be used to sustain the gospel laborers in their work. . . . Read carefully the third chapter of Malachi and see what God says about the tithe.—9T 249 (1909).

The New Testament does not re-enact the law of the tithe, as it does not that of the Sabbath; for the validity of both is assumed, and their deep spiritual import explained.—CS 66 (1882).

The Lord now calls upon Seventh-day Adventists in every locality to consecrate themselves to Him and to do their very best, according to their circumstances, to assist in His work. By their liberality in making gifts and offerings, He desires them to reveal their appreciation of His blessings and their gratitude for His mercy.—9T 132 (1909).

Dying charity is a poor substitute for living benevolence.—5T 155 (1882).

The wants of the cause will continually increase as we near the close of time.—5T 156 (1882).

We are placed on trial in this world, to determine our fitness for the future life. None can enter heaven whose characters are defiled by the foul blot of selfishness. Therefore, God tests us here, by committing to us temporal possessions, that our use of these may show whether we can be entrusted with eternal riches.—CS 22 (1893).

Establish New Institutions

Some may say, "If the Lord is coming soon, what need is there to establish schools, sanitariums, and food factories? What need is there for our young people to learn trades?"

It is the Lord's design that we shall constantly improve the talents He has given us. We cannot do this unless we use them. The prospect of Christ's soon coming should not lead us to idleness. Instead, it should lead us to do all we possibly can to bless and benefit humanity.—MM 268 (1902).

A great work must be done all through the world, and let no one conclude that because the end is near there is no need of special effort to build up the various institutions as the cause shall demand. . . . When the Lord shall bid us make no further effort to build meetinghouses and establish schools, sanitariums, and publishing institutions, it will be time for us to fold our hands and let the Lord close up the work, but now is our opportunity to show our zeal for God and our love for humanity.—6T 440 (1900).

Medical Missionary Work

As religious aggression subverts the liberties of our nation, those who would stand for freedom of conscience will be placed in unfavorable positions. For their own sake they should, while they have opportunity, become intelligent in regard to disease, its causes, prevention, and cure. And those who do this will find a field of labor anywhere. There will be suffering ones, plenty of them, who will need help, not only among those of our own faith but largely among those who know not the truth.—CH 506 (1892).

I wish to tell you that soon there will be no work done in ministerial lines but medical missionary work.—CH 533 (1901).

God's People Value Their Health

The health reform, I was shown, is a part of the third angel's message and is just as closely connected with it as are the arm and hand with the human body.—1T 486 (1867).

Tea, coffee, tobacco, and alcohol we must present as sinful indulgences. We cannot place on the same ground, meat, eggs, butter, cheese, and such articles placed upon the table. These are not to be borne in front, as the burden of our work. The former—tea, coffee, tobacco, beer, wine, and all spirituous liquors—are not to be taken moderately, but discarded.—3SM 287 (1881).

True temperance teaches us to dispense entirely with everything hurtful and to use judiciously that which is healthful.—PP 562 (1890).

Pure air, sunlight, abstemiousness, rest, exercise, proper diet, the use of water, trust in divine power— these are the true remedies.—MH 127 (1905).

Whatever injures the health not only lessens physical vigor but tends to weaken the mental and moral powers. Indulgence in any unhealthful practice makes it more difficult for one to discriminate between right and wrong and hence more difficult to resist evil. —MH 128 (1905).

Return to the Original Diet

God is trying to lead us back, step by step, to His original design—that man should subsist upon the natural products of the earth. Among those who are waiting for the coming of the Lord meat eating will eventually be done away; flesh will cease to form a part of their diet. We should ever keep this end in view and endeavor to work steadily toward it.—CH 450 (1890).

Greater reforms should be seen among the people who claim to be looking for the soon appearing of Christ. Health reform is to do among our people a work which it has not yet done. There are those who ought to be awake to the danger of meat eating who are still eating the flesh of animals, thus endangering the physical, mental, and spiritual health. Many who are now only half converted on the question of meat eating will go from God's people, to walk no more with them.—RH May 27, 1902.

Time for Fasting and Prayer

Now and onward till the close of time the people of God should be more earnest, more wide-awake, not trusting in their own wisdom, but in the wisdom of their Leader. They should set aside days for fasting and prayer. Entire abstinence from food may not be required, but they should eat sparingly of the most simple food.—CD 188, 189 (1904).

The true fasting which should be recommended to all is abstinence from every stimulating kind of food, and the proper use of wholesome, simple food, which God has provided in abundance. Men need to think less of what they shall eat and drink of temporal food, and much more in regard to the food from heaven, that will give tone and vitality to the whole religious experience.—MM 283 (1896).

The leaven of godliness has not entirely lost its power. At the time when the danger and depression of the church are greatest, the little company who are standing in the light will be sighing and crying for the abominations that are done in the land. But more especially will their prayers arise in behalf of the church because its members are doing after the manner of the world.—5T 209, 210 (1882).

Entire Trust in God

Because of unconsecrated workers, things will sometimes go wrong. You may weep over the result of the wrong course of others, but do not worry. The work is under the supervision of the blessed Master. All He asks is that the workers shall come to Him for their orders, and obey His directions. All parts of the work—our churches, missions, Sabbath schools, institutions—are carried upon His heart. Why worry? The intense longing to see the church imbued with life must be tempered with entire trust in God. . . .

Let no one overtax his God-given powers in an effort to advance the Lord's work more rapidly. The power of man cannot hasten the work; with this must be united the power of heavenly intelligences. . . . Though all the workmen now bearing the heaviest burdens should be laid aside, God's work would be carried forward.—7T 298 (1902).

Family Worship

Evening and morning join with your children in God's worship, reading His Word and singing His praise. Teach them to repeat God's law.—Ev 499 (1904).

Let the seasons of family worship be short and
spirited. Do not let your children or any member of
your family dread them because of their tediousness
or lack of interest. When a long chapter is read and
explained and a long prayer offered, this precious
service becomes wearisome, and it is a relief when it
is over. . . .

Let the father select a portion of Scripture that is
interesting and easily understood; a few verses will be
sufficient to furnish a lesson which may be studied
and practiced through the day. Questions may be
asked, a few earnest, interesting remarks made, or
[an] incident, short and to the point, may be brought
in by way of illustration. At least a few verses of
spirited song may be sung, and the prayer offered
should be short and pointed. The one who leads in
prayer should not pray about everything, but should
express his needs in simple words, and praise God
with thanksgiving.—CG 521, 522 (1884).

Guard Association With the World

[Rev. 18:1-3, quoted.] While this message is sound-
ing, while the proclamation of truth is doing its
separating work, we as faithful sentinels of God are to
discern what our real position is. We are not to
confederate with worldlings, lest we become imbued
with their spirit, lest our spiritual discernment become confused and we view those who have the truth
and bear the message of the Lord from the standpoint

of the professed Christian churches. At the same time we are not to be like the Pharisees and hold ourselves aloof from them.—EGW'88 1161 (1893).

Those who are watching and waiting for the appearing of Christ in the clouds of heaven will not be mingling with the world in pleasure societies and gatherings merely for their own amusement.—Ms 4, 1898.

To bind ourselves up by contracts or in partnerships or business associations with those not of our faith is not in the order of God.—RH Aug. 4, 1904.

We should unite with other people just as far as we can and not sacrifice principle. This does not mean that we should join their lodges and societies, but that we should let them know that we are most heartily in sympathy with the temperance question.—Te 220 (1884).

Recreation That Christ Approves

It is the privilege and duty of Christians to seek to refresh their spirits and invigorate their bodies by innocent recreation, with the purpose of using their physical and mental powers to the glory of God.—MYP 364 (1871).

Christians have many sources of happiness at their command, and they may tell with unerring accuracy what pleasures are lawful and right. They may enjoy such recreations as will not dissipate the mind or debase the soul, such as will not disappoint and leave a sad after-influence to destroy self-respect or bar the way to usefulness. If they can take Jesus with them and maintain a prayerful spirit they are perfectly safe.—MYP 38 (1884).

Our gatherings should be so conducted, and we should so conduct ourselves, that when we return to our homes we can have a conscience void of offense toward God and man, a consciousness that we have not wounded or injured in any manner those with whom we have been associated or had an injurious influence over them. . . .

Any amusement in which you can engage, asking the blessing of God upon it in faith, will not be dangerous. But any amusement which disqualifies you for secret prayer, for devotion at the altar of prayer, or for taking part in the prayer meeting, is not safe, but dangerous.—MYP 386 (1913).

Music That Elevates

As the children of Israel journeying through the wilderness cheered their way by the music of sacred song, so God bids His children today gladden their pilgrim life. There are few means more effective for fixing His words in the memory than repeating them in song. And such song has wonderful power. It has power to subdue rude and uncultivated natures, power to quicken thought and to awaken sympathy, to promote harmony of action, and to banish the gloom and foreboding that destroy courage and weaken effort.—Ed 167, 168 (1903).

Music forms a part of God's worship in the courts above, and we should endeavor in our songs of praise

to approach as nearly as possible to the harmony of
the heavenly choirs. . . . Singing, as a part of religious
service, is as much an act of worship as is prayer.
—PP 594 (1890).

The use of musical instruments is not at all objectionable. These were used in religious services in
ancient times. The worshipers praised God upon the
harp and cymbal, and music should have its place in
our services.—Ev 500, 501 (1898).

Television and the Theater

Among the most dangerous resorts for pleasure is
the theater. Instead of being a school of morality and
virtue, as is so often claimed, it is the very hotbed of
immorality. Vicious habits and sinful propensities are
strengthened and confirmed by these entertainments.
Low songs, lewd gestures, expressions, and attitudes,
deprave the imagination and debase the morals.

Every youth who habitually attends such exhibi-
tions will be corrupted in principle. There is no influence in our land more powerful to poison the imagination, to destroy religious impressions, and to blunt the
relish for the tranquil pleasures and sober realities of
life than theatrical amusements. The love for these
scenes increases with every indulgence, as the desire
for intoxicating drink strengthens with its use.—4T
652, 653 (1881).

The blessing of God would not be invoked upon the
hour spent at the theater or in the dance. No Christian

would wish to meet death in such a place. No one
would wish to be found there when Christ shall
come.—MYP 398 (1882).

The only safe amusements are such as will not
banish serious and religious thoughts. The only safe
places of resort are those to which we can take Jesus
with us.—OHC 284 (1883).

Dress and Adornments

There is no need to make the dress question the
main point of your religion. There is something richer
to speak of. Talk of Christ, and when the heart is
converted everything that is out of harmony with the
Word of God will drop off.—Ev 272 (1889).

If we are Christians, we shall follow Christ, even
though the path in which we are to walk cuts right
across our natural inclinations. There is no use in
telling you that you must not wear this or that, for if
the love of these vain things is in your heart your
laying off your adornments will only be like cutting
the foliage off a tree. The inclinations of the natural
heart would again assert themselves. You must have
a conscience of your own.—CG 429, 430 (1892).

I beg of our people to walk carefully and circum-
spectly before God. Follow the customs in dress so far
as they conform to health principles. Let our sisters
dress plainly, as many do, having the dress of good,
durable material, appropriate for this age, and let not

the dress question fill the mind. Our sisters should dress with simplicity. They should clothe themselves in modest apparel, with shamefacedness and sobriety. Give to the world a living illustration of the inward adorning of the grace of God.—3SM 242 (1897).

The outside appearance is an index to the heart. —1T 136 (1856).

The Need for Publications

Publications should be issued, written in the plainest, simplest language, explaining the subjects of vital interest, and making known the things that are to come upon the world.—HM Feb. 1, 1890.

The first and second messages were given in 1843 and 1844, and we are now under the proclamation of the third, but all three of the messages are still to be proclaimed. . . . These messages we are to give to the world in publications, in discourses, showing in the line of prophetic history the things that have been and the things that will be.—CW 26, 27 (1896).

Unvarnished truth must be spoken in leaflets and pamphlets, and these must be scattered like the leaves of autumn.—9T 230 (1897).

Patriarchs and Prophets, Daniel and the Revelation, and *The Great Controversy* are needed now as never before. They should be widely circulated because the truths they emphasize will open many blind eyes.—CM 123 (1905).

As long as probation continues there will be opportunity for the canvasser to work.—6T 478 (1900).

No Sharp Thrusts in Our Papers

Let not those who write for our papers make unkind thrusts and allusions that will certainly do harm and that will hedge up the way and hinder us from doing the work that we should do in order to reach all classes, the Catholics included. It is our work to speak the truth in love and not to mix in with the truth the unsanctified elements of the natural heart and speak things that savor of the same spirit possessed by our enemies. . . .

We are not to use harsh and cutting words. Keep them out of every article written, drop them out of every address given. Let the Word of God do the cutting, the rebuking; let finite men hide and abide in Jesus Christ.—9T 240, 241, 244 (1909).

We should weed out each expression in our writings, our utterances, that, if taken by itself, could be misinterpreted so as to make it seem antagonistic to law and order. Everything should be carefully considered lest we place ourselves on record as uttering things that will make us appear disloyal to our country and its laws.—Letter 36, 1895.

Christianity is not manifested in pugilistic accusations and condemnations.—6T 397 (1900).

Beware of Side Issues

God has not passed His people by and chosen one

solitary man here and another there as the only ones worthy to be entrusted with His truth. He does not give one man new light contrary to the established faith of the body. In every reform men have arisen making this claim. . . . Let none be self-confident, as though God had given them special light above their brethren. . . .

One accepts some new and original idea which does not seem to conflict with the truth. He . . . dwells upon it until it seems to him to be clothed with beauty and importance, for Satan has power to give this false appearance. At last it becomes the all-absorbing theme, the one great point around which everything centers, and the truth is uprooted from the heart. . . .

I warn you to beware of these side issues, whose tendency is to divert the mind from the truth. Error is never harmless. It never sanctifies, but always brings confusion and dissension.—5T 291, 292 (1885).

Emphasize Unity, Not Differences

There are a thousand temptations in disguise prepared for those who have the light of truth, and the only safety for any of us is in receiving no new doctrine, no new interpretation of the Scriptures, without first submitting it to brethren of experience. Lay it before them in a humble, teachable spirit, with earnest prayer, and if they see no light in it, yield to their judgment, for "in the multitude of counselors there is safety." . . .

Men and women will arise professing to have some new light or some new revelation whose tendency is to unsettle faith in the old landmarks. Their doctrines will not bear the test of God's Word, yet souls will be deceived. False reports will be circulated, and some will be taken in this snare. . . . We cannot be too watchful against every form of error, for Satan is constantly seeking to draw men from the truth.—5T 293, 295, 296 (1885).

We must make it appear essential to be united, not that we are to require others to come to our ideas, but if all are seeking the meekness and lowliness of Christ they will have the mind of Christ. Then there will be unity of spirit.—Letter 15, 1892.

I urge those who claim to believe the truth to walk in unity with their brethren. Do not seek to give to the world occasion to say that we are extremists, that we are disunited, that one teaches one thing, and one another. Avoid dissension.—TM 57 (1893).

How to Meet Critics

Those who have departed from the faith will come to our congregations to divert our attention from the work that God would have done. You cannot afford to turn your ears from the truth to fables. Do not stop to try to convert the one who is speaking words of reproach against your work, but let it be seen that you are inspired by the Spirit of Jesus Christ, and angels of God will put into your lips words that will reach the hearts of the opposers. If these men persist in pressing their way in, those who are of a sensible mind in the congregation will understand that yours is the higher standard. So speak that it will be known that Jesus Christ is speaking through you.—9T 148, 149 (1909).

Exalt the Word of God

If we work to create an excitement of feeling, we shall have all we want, and more than we can possibly know how to manage. Calmly and clearly "Preach the Word." We must not regard it as our work to create an excitement. The Holy Spirit of God alone can create a healthy enthusiasm. Let God work, and let the human agent walk softly before Him, watching, waiting, praying, looking unto Jesus every moment, led and controlled by the precious Spirit, which is light and life.—2SM 16, 17 (1894).

We must go to the people with the solid Word of God, and when they receive that Word, the Holy Spirit may come, but it always comes, as I have stated before, in a way that commends itself to the judgment of the people. In our speaking, our singing, and in all our spiritual exercises, we are to reveal that calmness and dignity and godly fear that actuates every true child of God.—2SM 43 (1908).

It is through the *Word*—not feeling, not excitement—that we want to influence the people to obey the truth. On the platform of God's Word we can stand with safety.—3SM 375 (1908).

7.

Country Living

The Divine Ideal

Although everything God had made was in the perfection of beauty, and there seemed nothing wanting upon the earth which God had created to make Adam and Eve happy, yet He manifested His great love to them by planting a garden especially for them. A portion of their time was to be occupied in the happy employment of dressing the garden, and a portion in receiving the visits of angels, listening to their instruction, and in happy meditation. Their labor was not wearisome, but pleasant and invigorating. This beautiful garden was to be their home, their special residence.—3SG 34 (1864).

What were the conditions chosen by the infinite Father for His Son? A secluded home in the Galilean hills; a household sustained by honest, self-respecting labor; a life of simplicity; daily conflict with difficulty and hardship; self-sacrifice, economy, and patient, gladsome service; the hour of study at His mother's side, with the open scroll of Scripture; the quiet of dawn or twilight in the green valley; the holy ministries of nature; the study of creation and providence;

and the soul's communion with God—these were the conditions and opportunities of the early life of Jesus. —MH 365, 366 (1905).

Away From the Cities

Get out of the cities as soon as possible and purchase a little piece of land where you can have a garden, where your children can watch the flowers growing and learn from them lessons of simplicity and purity.—2SM 356 (1903).

Out of the cities, is my message at this time. Be assured that the call is for our people to locate miles away from the large cities. One look at San Francisco as it is today would speak to your intelligent minds, showing you the necessity of getting out of the cities. . . .

The Lord calls for His people to locate away from the cities, for in such an hour as ye think not, fire and brimstone will be rained from heaven upon these cities. Proportionate to their sins will be their visitation. When one city is destroyed, let not our people regard this matter as a light affair, and think that they may, if favorable opportunity offers, build themselves homes in that same destroyed city. . . .

Let all who would understand the meaning of these things read the eleventh chapter of Revelation. Read every verse, and learn the things that are yet to take place in the cities. Read also the scenes portrayed in the eighteenth chapter of the same book.—MR 1518 (May 10, 1906).

Fathers and mothers who possess a piece of land
and a comfortable home are kings and queens.
—AH 141 (1894).

Cities to Be Worked From Outposts

As God's commandment-keeping people we must
leave the cities. As did Enoch, we must work in the
cities but not dwell in them.—Ev 77, 78 (1899).

The cities are to be worked from outposts. Said the
messenger of God, "Shall not the cities be warned?
Yes, not by God's people living in them but by their
visiting them, to warn them of what is coming upon
the earth."—2SM 358 (1902).

For years I have been given special light that we are
not to center our work in the cities. The turmoil and
confusion that fill these cities, the conditions brought
about by the labor unions and the strikes, would prove
a great hindrance to our work.—7T 84 (1902).

When iniquity abounds in a nation there is always
to be heard some voice giving warning and instruction, as the voice of Lot was heard in Sodom. Yet Lot
could have preserved his family from many evils had
he not made his home in this wicked, polluted city. All
that Lot and his family did in Sodom could have been
done by them even if they had lived in a place some
distance away from the city.—Ev 78 (1903).

For the present, some will be obliged to labor in
Chicago, but these should be preparing working cen-

ters in rural districts from which to work the city. The Lord would have His people looking about them and securing humble, inexpensive places as centers for their work. And from time to time larger places will come to their notice, which they will be able to secure at a surprisingly low price.—Ev 402 (1906).

Rich Blessings in a Natural Environment

We say again, "Out of the cities." Do not consider it a great deprivation that you must go into the hills and mountains, but seek for that retirement where you can be alone with God, to learn His will and way. . . .

I urge our people to make it their lifework to seek for spirituality. Christ is at the door. This is why I say to our people, "Do not consider it a privation when you are called to leave the cities and move out into the country places. Here there await rich blessings for those who will grasp them. By beholding the scenes of nature, the works of the Creator, by studying God's handiwork, imperceptibly you will be changed into the same image." —2SM 355, 356 (1908).

Character Development
Easier in the Country

Parents flock with their families to the cities because they fancy it easier to obtain a livelihood there than in the country. The children, having nothing to do when not in school, obtain a street education. From evil associates they acquire habits of vice and dissipation.—5T 232 (1882).

Send the children to schools located in the city, where every phase of temptation is waiting to attract and demoralize them, and the work of character building is tenfold harder for both parents and children.—FE 326 (1894).

The cities are filled with temptation. We should plan our work in such a way as to keep our young people as far as possible from this contamination.—AH 136 (1902).

It is time for our people to take their families from the cities into more retired localities, else many of the youth, and many also of those older in years, will be ensnared and taken by the enemy.—8T 101 (1904).

There is not one family in a hundred who will be improved physically, mentally, or spiritually, by residing in the city. Faith, hope, love, happiness, can far better be gained in retired places, where there are fields and hills and trees. Take your children away from the sights and sounds of the city, away from the rattle and din of streetcars and teams, and their minds will become more healthy. It will be found easier to bring home to their hearts the truth of the Word of God.—AH 137 (1905).

Better Physical Health in Rural Environment

It is not God's will that His people shall settle in the cities, where there is constant turmoil and confusion. Their children should be spared this, for the whole system is demoralized by the hurry and rush and noise.—2 SM 357 (1902).

To many of those living in the cities who have not a spot of green grass to set their feet upon, who year after year have looked out upon filthy courts and narrow alleys, brick walls and pavements and skies clouded with dust and smoke—if these could be taken to some farming district, surrounded with the green fields, the woods and hills and brooks, the clear skies and the fresh, pure air of the country, it would seem almost like heaven.—MH 191, 192 (1905).

The physical surroundings in the cities are often a peril to health. The constant liability to contact with disease, the prevalence of foul air, impure water, impure food, the crowded, dark, unhealthful dwellings, are some of the many evils to be met. It was not God's purpose that people should be crowded into cities, huddled together in terraces and tenements. —MH 365 (1905).

Raise Your Own Provisions

The Lord desires His people to move into the country, where they can settle on the land, and raise their own fruit and vegetables, and where their children can be brought in direct contact with the works of God in nature. Take your families away from the cities, is my message.—2 SM 357, 358 (1902).

Again and again the Lord has instructed that our people are to take their families away from the cities, into the country, where they can raise their own provisions, for in the future the problem of buying and selling will be a very serious one. We should now begin to heed the instruction given us over and over again: Get out of the cities into rural districts, where the houses are not crowded closely together, and where you will be free from the interference of enemies. —2SM 141 (1904).

Locate Institutions "Just Out From the Large Cities"

Let men of sound judgment be appointed, not to publish abroad their intentions, but to search for such properties in the rural districts, in easy access to the cities, suitable for small training schools for workers, and where facilities may also be provided for treating the sick and weary souls who know not the truth. Look for such places just out from the large cities, where suitable buildings may be secured, either as a gift from the owners or purchased at a reasonable price by the gifts of our people. Do not erect buildings in the noisy cities.—Ev 77 (1909).

Cooranbong, New South Wales

Where shall our Australian Bible School be located? ... Should schools be located in the cities or within a few miles from them it would be most difficult to counteract the influence of the former education which students have received in regard to these holidays and the practices connected with them, such as horse racing, betting, and the offering of prizes. ...

We shall find it necessary to establish our schools out of, and away from, the cities, and yet not so far away that they cannot be in touch with them, to do them good, to let light shine amid the moral darkness.—FE 310, 313 (1894).

Everything about the place had impressed me favorably except the fact that we were far from the great thoroughfares of travel, and therefore would not have an opportunity of letting our light shine amid the moral darkness that covers our large cities like the pall of death. This seems the only objection that presents itself to my mind. But then, it would not be advisable to establish our school in any of our large cities.—8MR 137 (1894).

I am more than ever convinced that this is the right location for the school.—8MR 360 (1894).

Huntsville, Alabama

Those who have charge of the schoolwork at Graysville[1] and Huntsville should see what can be done by these institutions to establish such industries, so that our people desiring to leave the cities can obtain modest homes without a large outlay of means, and can also find employment.—Letter 25, 1902.

---

1. The property at Graysville, Tennessee, fifty miles north of Chattanooga, consisted of nine acres of land adjacent to a village of about 200 people. The school was moved to its present location at Collegedale in 1916.

It was in the providence of God that the Huntsville School farm was purchased. It is in a good locality. Near it there are large nurseries, and in these nurseries some of the students have worked during the summer to earn money to pay their expense at the Huntsville School.—SpT-B(12) 11 (1904).

The Huntsville School farm is a most beautiful place, and with its three hundred and more acres of land, should accomplish much in the line of industrial training and the raising of crops.—SpT-B(12x) 13 (1904).

Recently the question was asked me, "Would it not be well to sell the school land at Huntsville, and buy a smaller place?" Instruction was given me that this farm must not be sold, that the situation possesses many advantages for the carrying forward of a colored school.—SpM 359 (1904).

Berrien Springs, Michigan

I hear that there is some thought of locating the school at Berrien Springs in the southwest of Michigan. I am much pleased with the description of this place. . . . In such a place as Berrien Springs the school can be made an object lesson, and I hope that no one will interpose to prevent the carrying forward of this work.—4MR 407 (July 12, 1901).

The good hand of the Lord has been with our people in the selection of a place for the school. This place corresponds to the representations given me as to where the school should be located. It is away from the cities, and there is an abundance of land for agricultural purposes, and room so that houses will not need to be built one close to another. There is plenty of ground where students may be educated in the cultivation of the soil.—RH Jan. 28, 1902.

In moving the college from Battle Creek and establishing it in Berrien Springs, Brethren Magan and Sutherland have acted in harmony with the light that God gave. They have worked hard under great difficulties. . . . God has been with them. He has approved of their efforts.—4MR 260, 261 (1904).

Stoneham, Massachusetts

The Lord in His providence has opened the way for His workers to take an advance step in New England—a field where much special work should be done. The brethren there have been enabled to arrange to change the location of the sanitarium from South Lancaster to Melrose, a place much nearer Boston, and yet far enough removed from the busy city so that the patients may have the most favorable conditions for recovery of health. The transfer of the New England Sanitarium to a place so convenient to the city of Boston is in God's providence.

When the Lord sets His hand to prepare the way before us, God forbid that any should stand back, questioning the wisdom of going forward or refusing to give encouragement and help. The removal of the

New England Sanitarium from South Lancaster to Melrose has been presented to me as being directed by the Lord.—SpT-B(13) 3 (1902).

Takoma Park, Washington, D.C.

The location that has been secured for our school and sanitarium is all that could be desired. The land resembles representations that have been shown me by the Lord. It is well adapted for the purpose for which it is to be used. There is on it ample room for a school and sanitarium without crowding either institution. The atmosphere is pure and the water is pure. A beautiful stream runs right through our land from north to south. This stream is a treasure more valuable than gold or silver. The building sites are upon fine elevations with excellent drainage.

One day we took a long drive through various parts of Takoma Park. A large part of the township is a natural forest. The houses are not small and crowded closely together, but are roomy and comfortable. They are surrounded by thrifty, second-growth pines, oaks, maples and other beautiful trees. The owners of these homes are mostly business men, many of them clerks in the government offices in Washington. They go to the city daily, returning in the evening to their quiet homes.

A good location for the printing office has been chosen, within easy distance of the post office, and a site for a meetinghouse also has been found. It seems as if Takoma Park has been specially prepared for us, and that it has been waiting to be occupied by our institutions and their workers.—ST June 15, 1904.

The Lord has opened this matter to me decidedly.
The publishing work that has been carried on in Battle
Creek should for the present be carried on near Wash-
ington. If after a time the Lord says, Move away from
Washington, we are to move.—RH Aug. 11, 1903.

Madison, Tennessee

I was surprised when, in speaking of the work they
wished to do in the South, they spoke of establishing
a school in some place a long way from Nashville.
From the light given me I knew that this would not be
the right thing to do, and I told them so. The work that
these brethren [E. A. Sutherland and P. T. Magan]
can do, because of the experience gained at Berrien
Springs, is to be carried on within easy access of
Nashville, for Nashville has not yet been worked as it
should be. And it will be a great blessing to the
workers in the school to be near enough to Nashville
to be able to counsel with the workers there.

In searching for a place for the school the brethren
found a farm of four hundred acres for sale about nine
miles from Nashville. The size of the farm, its situation,
the distance that it is from Nashville, and the moderate
sum for which it could be purchased, seemed to point it
out as the very place for the school work. We advised
that this place be purchased. I knew that all the land
would ultimately be needed.—RH Aug. 18, 1904.

Mountain View, California

Instruction has also been given that the Pacific
Press should be moved from Oakland. As the years

have passed by the city has grown, and it is now necessary to establish the printing plant in some more rural place, where land can be secured for the homes of the employees. Those who are connected with our offices of publication should not be obliged to live in the crowded cities. They should have opportunity to obtain homes where they will be able to live without requiring high wages.—FE 492 (1904).

Mountain View is a town which has many advantages. It is surrounded by beautiful orchards. The climate is mild and fruit and vegetables of all kinds can be grown. The town is not large, yet it has electric lights, mail carriers, and many other advantages usually seen only in cities.—Letter 141, 1904.

Some have wondered why our office of publication should be moved from Oakland to Mountain View. God has been calling upon His people to leave the cities. The youth who are connected with our institutions should not be exposed to the temptations and the corruption to be found in the large cities. Mountain View has seemed to be a favorable location for the printing office.—CL 29 (1905).

Loma Linda, California

We thank the Lord that we have a good sanitarium at Paradise Valley, seven miles from San Diego; a sanitarium at Glendale, eight miles from Los Angeles; and a large and beautiful place at Loma Linda, sixty-two miles east from Los Angeles, and close to Redlands,

Riverside, and San Bernardino. The Loma Linda property is one of the most beautiful sanitarium sites I have ever seen.—LLM 141 (1905).

Loma Linda is a place that the Lord has especially designated as a center for the training of medical missionaries.—Letter 188, 1907.

Here there are wonderful advantages for a school. The farm, the orchard, the pasture land, the large buildings, the ample grounds, the beauty—all are a great blessing.—LLM 310 (1907).

This place, Loma Linda, has wonderful advantages, and if those who are here will faithfully avail themselves of the advantages to become true medical missionaries they will let their light shine forth to those that are around them. We must seek God daily for His wisdom to be imparted to us.—Letter 374, 1907.

Here we have ideal advantages for a school and for a sanitarium. Here are advantages for the students and great advantages for the patients. I have been instructed that here we should have a school, conducted on the principles of the ancient schools of the prophets. . . . Physicians are to receive their education here.—MM 75, 76 (1907).

Angwin, California

As I have looked over this property I pronounce it to be superior in many respects. The school could not be located in a better spot. It is eight miles from St. Helena, and is free from city temptations. . . .

In time, more cottages will have to be built for the students, and these the students themselves can erect under the instruction of capable teachers. Timber can be prepared right on the ground for this work, and the students can be taught how to build in a creditable manner.

We need have no fear of drinking impure water for here it is supplied freely to us from the Lord's treasure house. I do not know how to be grateful enough for these many advantages. . . .

We realize that the Lord knew what we needed and that it is His providence that brought us here. . . . God wanted us here and He has placed us here. I was sure of this as I came on these grounds. . . . I believe that as you walk through these grounds you will come to the same decision—that the Lord designed this place for us.—1MR 340, 341, 343 (1909).

8.

The Cities

The Original City Builders

Upon receiving the curse of God, Cain had withdrawn from his father's household. He had first chosen his occupation as a tiller of the soil, and he now founded a city, calling it after the name of his eldest son [Gen. 4:17]. He had gone out from the presence of the Lord, cast away the promise of the restored Eden, to seek his possessions and enjoyment in the earth under the curse of sin, thus standing at the head of that great class of men who worship the god of this world.—PP 81 (1890).

For a time the descendants of Noah continued to dwell among the mountains where the ark had rested. As their numbers increased, apostasy soon led to division. Those who desired to forget their Creator and to cast off the restraint of His law felt a constant annoyance from the teaching and example of their God-fearing associates, and after a time they decided to separate from the worshipers of God. Accordingly they journeyed to the plain of Shinar, on the banks of the river Euphrates. . . .

Here they decided to build a city, and in it a tower of such stupendous height as should render it the wonder of the world [Gen. 11:2-4].—PP 118, 119 (1890).

The Cities Are Hotbeds of Vice

The pursuit of pleasure and amusement centers in the cities. Many parents who choose a city home for their children, thinking to give them greater advantages, meet with disappointment, and too late repent their terrible mistake. The cities of today are fast becoming like Sodom and Gomorrah. The many holidays encourage idleness. The exciting sports—theater-going, horse-racing, gambling, liquor-drinking, and reveling—stimulate every passion to intense activity. The youth are swept away by the popular current. —COL 54 (1900).

Light has been given me that the cities will be filled with confusion, violence, and crime, and that these things will increase till the end of this earth's history.—7T 84 (1902).

The world over, cities are becoming hotbeds of vice. On every hand are the sights and sounds of evil. Everywhere are enticements to sensuality and dissipation.—MH 363 (1905).

Judgments Coming on the Cities

Terrible shocks will come upon the earth, and the lordly palaces erected at great expense will certainly become heaps of ruins.—3MR 312 (1891).

When God's restraining hand is removed, the destroyer begins his work. Then in our cities the greatest calamities will come.—3MR 314 (1897).

The Lord gives warnings to the inhabitants of the earth, as in the Chicago fire and the fires in Melbourne, London, and the city of New York.—Ms 127, 1897.

The end is near and every city is to be turned upside down every way. There will be confusion in every city. Everything that can be shaken is to be shaken and we do not know what will come next. The judgments will be according to the wickedness of the people and the light of truth that they have had.—1MR 248 (1902).

O that God's people had a sense of the impending destruction of thousands of cities, now almost given to idolatry.—Ev 29 (1903).

The time is near when large cities will be swept away, and all should be warned of these coming judgments.—Ev 29 (1910).

Catastrophe-proof
Buildings Will Become Ashes

I have seen the most costly structures in buildings erected and supposed to be fireproof, and just as Sodom perished in the flames of God's vengeance so will these proud structures become ashes. . . . The flattering monuments of men's greatness will be crumbled in the dust even before the last great destruction comes upon the world.—3SM 418 (1901).

God is withdrawing His Spirit from the wicked cities, which have become as the cities of the antediluvian world and as Sodom and Gomorrah. . . . Costly mansions, marvels of architectural skill, will be destroyed without a moment's notice when the Lord sees that the owners have passed the boundaries of forgiveness. The destruction by fire of the stately buildings, supposed to be fireproof, is an illustration of how in a short time earth's architecture will lie in ruins.—TDG 152 (1902).

Men will continue to erect expensive buildings, costing millions of money. Special attention will be called to their architectural beauty and the firmness and solidity with which they are constructed, but the Lord has instructed me that despite the unusual firmness and expensive display, these buildings will share the fate of the temple in Jerusalem.—5BC 1098 (1906).

New York City

God has not executed His wrath without mercy. His hand is stretched out still. His message must be given in Greater New York. The people must be shown how it is possible for God, by a touch of His hand, to destroy the property they have gathered together against the last great day.—3MR 310, 311 (1902).

I have no light in particular in regard to what is coming on New York, only that I know that one day the great buildings there will be thrown down by the turning and overturning of God's power. . . . Death will come in all places. *This is why I am so anxious for our cities to be warned.*—RH July 5, 1906.

On one occasion, when in New York City, I was in the night season called upon to behold buildings rising story after story toward heaven. These buildings were warranted to be fireproof, and they were erected to glorify their owners and builders. . . .

The scene that next passed before me was an alarm of fire. Men looked at the lofty and supposedly fireproof buildings and said: "They are perfectly safe." But these buildings were consumed as if made of pitch. The fire engines could do nothing to stay the destruction. The firemen were unable to operate the engines.—9T 12, 13 (1909).

Chicago and Los Angeles

Scenes that would soon take place in Chicago and other large cities also passed before me. As wickedness increased and the protecting power of God was withdrawn there were destructive winds and tempests. Buildings were destroyed by fire and shaken down by earthquakes. . . .

Some time after this I was shown that the vision of buildings in Chicago and the draft upon the means of our people to erect them, and their destruction, was an object lesson for our people, warning them not to invest largely of their means in property in Chicago, or any other city, unless the providence of God should positively open the way and plainly point out duty to build or buy as necessary in giving the note of warning. A similar caution was given in regard to building in Los Angeles. Repeatedly I have been instructed that we must not invest means in the erection of expensive buildings in cities.—PC 50 (1906).

San Francisco and Oakland

San Francisco and Oakland are becoming as Sodom and Gomorrah, and the Lord will visit them. Not far hence they will suffer under His judgments.—Ms 30, 1903.

The terrible earthquake that has visited San Francisco[1] will be followed by other manifestations of the power of God. His law has been transgressed. Cities have become polluted with sin. Study the history of Nineveh. God sent a special message by Jonah to that wicked city. . . . Many such messages as his would be given in our age, if the wicked cities would repent as did Nineveh.—Ms 61a, June 3, 1906.

Even in the cities where the judgments of God have fallen in consequence of such transgression there is no sign of repentance. The saloons are still open, and many temptations are kept before the people.—Letter 268, Aug. 20, 1906.

Other Wicked Cities

As we near the close of this earth's history, we shall have the scenes of the San Francisco calamity re-

---

1. The San Francisco earthquake and fire of April 18-19, 1906, left 503 dead and resulted in an estimated $350 million in property damage.

peated in other places. . . . These things make me feel
very solemn because I know that the judgment day is
right upon us. The judgments that have already come
are a warning, but not the finishing, of the punishment that will come on wicked cities. . . .

[Hab. 2:1-20; Zeph. 1:1-3:20; Zech. 1:1-4:14; Mal.
1:1-4, quoted.] These scenes will soon be witnessed,
just as they are clearly described. I present these
wonderful statements from the Scriptures for the
consideration of everyone. The prophecies recorded in
the Old Testament are the word of the Lord for the last
days, and will be fulfilled as surely as we have seen the
desolation of San Francisco.—Letter 154, May 26,
1906.

I am bidden to declare the message that cities full
of transgression, and sinful in the extreme, will be
destroyed by earthquakes, by fire, by flood.—Ev 27
(April 27, 1906).

All the warnings of Christ regarding the events
that will occur near the close of this earth's history are
now being fulfilled in our large cities. God is permitting these things to be brought to light that he who
runs may read. The city of San Francisco is a sample
of what the whole world is becoming. The wicked
bribery, the misappropriation of means, the fraudulent transactions among men who have power to
release the guilty and condemn the innocent—all this
iniquity is filling other large cities of the earth and is
making the world as it was in the days that were
before the Flood.—Letter 230, 1907.

Labor Unions in the Cities

Satan is busily at work in our crowded cities. His work is to be seen in the confusion, the strife and discord between labor and capital, and the hypocrisy that has come into the churches. . . . The lust of the flesh, the pride of the eyes, the display of selfishness, the misuse of power, the cruelty and the force used to cause men to unite with confederacies and unions—binding themselves up in bundles for the burning of the great fires of the last days—all these are the working of satanic agencies.—Ev 26 (1903).

The wicked are being bound up in bundles, bound up in trusts, in unions, in confederacies. Let us have nothing to do with these organizations. God is our Ruler, our Governor, and He calls us to come out from the world and be separate. "Come out from among them, and be ye separate, saith the Lord, and touch not the unclean thing" [2 Cor. 6:17]. If we refuse to do this, if we continue to link up with the world and to look at every matter from a worldly standpoint, we shall become like the world. When worldly policy and worldly ideas govern our transactions we cannot stand on the high and holy platform of eternal truth.—4BC 1142 (1903).

Labor Unions
a Source of Trouble for Adventists

The trades unions will be one of the agencies that will bring upon this earth a time of trouble such as has not been since the world began. . . .

A few men will combine to grasp all the means to be obtained in certain lines of business. Trades unions will be formed, and those who refuse to join these unions will be marked men. . . .

Because of these unions and confederacies, it will soon be very difficult for our institutions to carry on their work in the cities. My warning is: Keep out of the cities. Build no sanitariums in the cities.—2SM 142 (1903).

The time is fast coming when the controlling power of the labor unions will be very oppressive.—2SM 141 (1904).

Many in the Cities Long for Light and Truth

Strictly will the cities of the nations be dealt with, and yet they will not be visited in the extreme of God's indignation, because some souls will yet break away from the delusions of the enemy and will repent and be converted.—Ev 27 (1906).

The spiritual darkness that covers the whole world is intensified in the crowded centers of population. It is in the cities of the nations that the gospel worker finds the greatest impenitence and the greatest need. And in these same cities are presented to soul-winners some of the greatest opportunities. Mingled with the multitudes who have no thought of God and heaven are many who long for light and for purity of heart. Even among the careless and indifferent there are not a few whose attention may be arrested by a revelation of God's love for the human soul.—RH Nov. 17, 1910.

Earnest Effort Needed in the Cities

In preparation for the coming of our Lord, we are to do a large work in the great cities. We have a solemn testimony to bear in these great centers.—*Words of Encouragement to Self-supporting Workers* (Ph 113) 5 (1909).

The warning message for this time is not being given earnestly in the great business world. Day after day the centers of commerce and trade are thronged with men and women who need the truth for this time but who gain no saving knowledge of its precious principles because earnest, persevering efforts are not put forth to reach this class of people where they are.—CW 14 (1909).

The third angel's message is now to be proclaimed, not only in far-off lands, but in neglected places close by, where multitudes dwell unwarned and unsaved. Our cities everywhere are calling for earnest, whole-hearted labor from the servants of God.—RH Nov. 17, 1910.

Not All Can Leave the Cities Yet

Whenever possible, it is the duty of parents to make homes in the country for their children.—AH 141 (1906).

More and more, as time advances, our people will have to leave the cities. For years we have been instructed that our brethren and sisters, and especially families with children, should plan to leave the cities as the way opens before them to do so. Many will have to labor earnestly to help open the way. But until it is possible for them to leave, so long as they remain, they should be most active in doing missionary work, however limited their sphere of influence may be. —2SM 360 (1906).

Our cities are increasing in wickedness, and it is becoming more and more evident that those who remain in them unnecessarily do so at the peril of their soul's salvation.—CL 9 (1907).

Cities and towns are steeped in sin and moral corruption, yet there are Lots in every Sodom.—6T 136 (1900).

Schools, Churches, Restaurants Needed in the Cities

Much more can be done to save and educate the children of those who at present cannot get away from the cities. This is a matter worthy of our best efforts. Church schools are to be established for the children in the cities, and in connection with these schools provision is to be made for the teaching of higher studies, where these are called for.—CG 306 (1903).

Our restaurants must be in the cities, for otherwise the workers in these restaurants could not reach the people and teach them the principles of right living. —2SM 142 (1903).

Repeatedly the Lord has instructed us that we are to work the cities from outpost centers. In these cities we are to have houses of worship, as memorials for God, but institutions for the publication of our literature, for the healing of the sick, and for the training of workers [colleges], are to be established outside the cities. Especially is it important that our youth be shielded from the temptations of city life.—2SM 358 (1907).

Precipitous Moves
to the Country Not Advised

Let everyone take time to consider carefully and not be like the man in the parable who began to build and was not able to finish. Not a move should be made but that movement and all that it portends are carefully considered—everything weighed. . . .

There may be individuals who will make a rush to do something, and enter into some business they know nothing about. This God does not require. . . .

Let there be nothing done in a disorderly manner, that there shall be a great loss or sacrifice made upon property because of ardent, impulsive speeches which stir up an enthusiasm which is not after the order of God, that a victory that was essential to be gained, shall, for lack of level-headed moderation and proper contemplation and sound principles and purposes, be turned into a defeat.[2]—2SM 362, 363 (1893).

---

2. Written December 22, 1893, in reply to a letter from a leading worker in Battle Creek who had informed Mrs. White that, in response to her urging, "between one and two hundred" were preparing to leave the city for a rural location "as soon as possible." See *Selected Messages*, book 2, pp. 361-364.

The Signal for Flight From the Cities

The time is not far distant when, like the early disciples, we shall be forced to seek a refuge in desolate and solitary places. As the siege of Jerusalem by the Roman armies was the signal for flight to the Judean Christians, so the assumption of power on the part of our nation, in the decree enforcing the papal sabbath, will be a warning to us. It will then be time to leave the large cities, preparatory to leaving the smaller ones for retired homes in secluded places among the mountains.—5T 464, 465 (1885).

Some Righteous Still in the Cities
After the Death Decree Has Been Passed

In the time of trouble we all fled from the cities and villages but were pursued by the wicked, who entered the houses of the saints with a sword.—EW 34 (1851).

As the saints left the cities and villages they were pursued by the wicked, who sought to slay them. But the swords that were raised to kill God's people broke and fell as powerless as a straw. Angels of God shielded the saints.—EW 284, 285 (1858).

Though a general decree has fixed the time when commandment-keepers may be put to death, their enemies will in some cases anticipate the decree, and before the time specified will endeavor to take their lives. But none can pass the mighty guardians stationed about every faithful soul. Some are assailed in their flight from the cities and villages, but the swords raised against them break and fall as powerless as a straw. Others are defended by angels in the form of men of war.—GC 631 (1911).

9.

Sunday Laws

Satan's Challenge to God's Authority

God denounces Babylon "because she made all nations drink of the wine of the wrath of her fornication.". . .

God made the world in six days and rested on the seventh, sanctifying this day, and setting it apart from all others as holy to Himself, to be observed by His people throughout their generations. But the man of sin, exalting himself above God, sitting in the temple of God, and showing himself to be God, *thought* to change times and laws. This power, thinking to prove that it was not only equal to God, but above God, changed the rest day, placing the first day of the week where the seventh should be. And the Protestant world has taken this child of the papacy to be regarded as sacred. In the Word of God this is called her fornication [Rev. 14:8].—7BC 979 (1900).

During the Christian dispensation the great enemy of man's happiness has made the Sabbath of the fourth commandment an object of special attack. Satan says, "I will work at cross purposes with God. I will empower my followers to set aside God's memorial, the seventh-day Sabbath. Thus I will show the world that the day sanctified and blessed by God has been changed. That day shall not live in the minds of the people. I will obliterate the memory of it. I will place in its stead a day that does not bear the credentials of God, a day that cannot be a sign between God and His people. I will lead those who accept this day to place upon it the sanctity that God placed upon the seventh day."—PK 183, 184 (c. 1914).

The Sabbath the Great Point at Issue

In the warfare to be waged in the last days there will be united, in opposition to God's people, all the corrupt powers that have apostatized from allegiance to the law of Jehovah. In this warfare the Sabbath of the fourth commandment will be the great point at issue, for in the Sabbath commandment the great Lawgiver identifies Himself as the Creator of the heavens and the earth.—3SM 392 (1891).

"Verily My Sabbaths ye shall keep," the Lord says, "for it is a sign between Me and you throughout your generations; that ye may know that I am the Lord that doth sanctify you" (Ex. 31:13). Some will seek to place obstacles in the way of Sabbath observance, saying, "You do not know what day is the Sabbath," but they seem to understand when Sunday comes, and have manifested great zeal in making laws compelling its observance.—KC 148 (1900).

The Sunday-Law Movement in the 1880s[1]

We have been looking many years for a Sunday law to be enacted in our land, and now that the movement is right upon us, we ask, What are our people going to do in the matter? . . . We should especially seek God for grace and power to be given His people now. God lives, and we do not believe that the time has fully come when He would have our liberties restricted.

The prophet saw "four angels standing on the four corners of the earth, holding the four winds of the earth, that the wind should not blow on the earth, nor on the sea, nor on any tree." Another angel, ascending from the east, cried to them, saying, "Hurt not the earth, neither the sea, nor the trees, till we have sealed the servants of our God in their foreheads." This points out the work we now have to do, which is to cry to God for the angels to hold the four winds until missionaries shall be sent to all parts of the world, and shall have proclaimed the warning against disobeying the law of Jehovah.—RH Extra, Dec. 11, 1888.

Sunday-Law Advocates
Do Not Realize What They Are Doing

The Sunday movement is now making its way in darkness. The leaders are concealing the true issue, and many who unite in the movement do not themselves see whither the undercurrent is tending. . . .

---

1. For helpful background information and more extensive E. G. White quotations, see *Selected Messages*, book 3, pp. 380-402, and *Testimonies for the Church*, vol. 5, pp. 711-718.

They are working in blindness. They do not see that if a Protestant government sacrifices the principles that have made them a free, independent nation, and through legislation brings into the Constitution principles that will propagate papal falsehood and papal delusion, they are plunging into the Roman horrors of the Dark Ages.—RH Extra, Dec. 11, 1888.

There are many, even of those engaged in this movement for Sunday enforcement, who are blinded to the results which will follow this action. They do not see that they are striking directly against religious liberty. There are many who have never understood the claims of the Bible Sabbath and the false foundation upon which the Sunday institution rests. . . .

Those who are making an effort to change the Constitution and secure a law enforcing Sunday observance little realize what will be the result. A crisis is just upon us.—5T 711, 753 (1889).

Not to Sit in Quietude, Doing Nothing

It is our duty to do all in our power to avert the threatened danger. . . . A vast responsibility is devolving upon men and women of prayer throughout the land to petition that God may sweep back this cloud of evil, and give a few more years of grace to work for the Master.—RH Extra, Dec. 11, 1888.

Those who are now keeping the commandments of God need to bestir themselves that they may obtain the special help which God alone can give them. They should work more earnestly to delay as long as possible the threatened calamity.—RH Dec. 18, 1888.

Let not the commandment-keeping people of God be silent at this time as though we gracefully accepted the situation.—7BC 975 (1889).

We are not doing the will of God if we sit in quietude, doing nothing to preserve liberty of conscience. Fervent, effectual prayer should be ascending to heaven that this calamity may be deferred until we can accomplish the work which has so long been neglected. Let there be most earnest prayer and then let us work in harmony with our prayers.—5T 714 (1889).

There are many who are at ease, who are, as it were, asleep. They say, "If prophecy has foretold the enforcement of Sunday observance the law will surely be enacted," and having come to this conclusion they sit down in a calm expectation of the event, comforting themselves with the thought that God will protect His people in the day of trouble. But God will not save us if we make no effort to do the work He has committed to our charge. . . .

As faithful watchmen you should see the sword coming and give the warning, that men and women may not pursue a course through ignorance that they would avoid if they knew the truth.—RH Extra, Dec. 24, 1889.

Oppose Sunday Laws by Pen and Vote

We cannot labor to please men who will use their influence to repress religious liberty and to set in operation oppressive measures to lead or compel their fellow men to keep Sunday as the Sabbath. The first day of the week is not a day to be reverenced. It is a spurious sabbath, and the members of the Lord's family cannot participate with the men who exalt this day and violate the law of God by trampling upon His Sabbath. The people of God are not to vote to place such men in office, for when they do this they are partakers with them of the sins which they commit while in office.—FE 475 (1899).

I do hope that the trumpet will give a certain sound in regard to this Sunday-law movement. I think that it would be best if in our papers the subject of the perpetuity of the law of God were made a specialty. . . . We should now be doing our very best to defeat this Sunday law.—CW 97, 98 (1906).

The United States Will Pass a Sunday Law

When our nation shall so abjure the principles of its government as to enact a Sunday law, Protestantism will in this act join hands with popery.—5T 712 (1889).

Protestants will throw their whole influence and strength on the side of the papacy. By a national act enforcing the false sabbath they will give life and vigor to the corrupt faith of Rome, reviving her tyranny and oppression of conscience.—Mar 179 (1893).

Sooner or later Sunday laws will be passed.—RH Feb. 16, 1905.

Soon the Sunday laws will be enforced, and men in positions of trust will be embittered against the little handful of God's commandment-keeping people. —4MR 278 (1909).

The prophecy of Revelation 13 declares that the power represented by the beast with lamblike horns shall cause "the earth and them which dwell therein" to worship the papacy—there symbolized by the beast "like unto a leopard." . . . This prophecy will be fulfilled when the United States shall enforce Sunday observance, which Rome claims as the special acknowledgment of her supremacy. . . .

Political corruption is destroying love of justice and regard for truth, and even in free America rulers and legislators, in order to secure public favor, will yield to the popular demand for a law enforcing Sunday observance.—GC 578, 579, 592 (1911).

Arguments Used by Sunday-Law Advocates

Satan puts his interpretation upon events, and they think, as he would have them, that the calamities which fill the land are a result of Sundaybreaking. Thinking to appease the wrath of God these influential men make laws enforcing Sunday observance. —10MR 239 (1899).

This very class put forth the claim that the fast-spreading corruption is largely attributable to the desecration of the so-called "Christian sabbath" and that the enforcement of Sunday observance would greatly improve the morals of society. This claim is especially urged in America, where the doctrine of the true Sabbath has been most widely preached.—GC 587 (1911).

Protestantism and Catholicism Act in Concert

Protestantism shall give the hand of fellowship to the Roman power. Then there will be a law against the Sabbath of God's creation, and then it is that God will do His "strange work" in the earth.—7BC 910 (1886).

How the Roman church can clear herself from the charge of idolatry we cannot see. . . . And this is the religion which Protestants are beginning to look upon with so much favor, and which will eventually be united with Protestantism. This union will not, however, be effected by a change in Catholicism, for Rome never changes. She claims infallibility. It is Protestantism that will change. The adoption of liberal ideas on its part will bring it where it can clasp the hand of Catholicism.—RH June 1, 1886.

The professed Protestant world will form a confederacy with the man of sin, and the church and the world will be in corrupt harmony.—7BC 975 (1891).

Romanism in the Old World, and apostate Protestantism in the New, will pursue a similar course toward those who honor all the divine precepts.—GC 616 (1911).

Sunday Laws Honor Rome

When the leading churches of the United States, uniting upon such points of doctrine as are held by them in common, shall influence the state to enforce their decrees and to sustain their institutions, then Protestant America will have formed an image of the Roman hierarchy, and the infliction of civil penalties upon dissenters will inevitably result. . . .

The enforcement of Sundaykeeping on the part of Protestant churches is an enforcement of the worship of the papacy. . . .

In the very act of enforcing a religious duty by secular power, the churches would themselves form an image to the beast; hence the enforcement of Sundaykeeping in the United States would be an enforcement of the worship of the beast and his image.—GC 445, 448, 449 (1911).

When Protestantism shall stretch her hand across the gulf to grasp the hand of the Roman power, when she shall reach over the abyss to clasp hands with spiritualism, when, under the influence of this three-fold union, our country shall repudiate every principle of its Constitution as a Protestant and republican government and shall make provision for the propaga-tion of papal falsehoods and delusions, then we may know that the time has come for the marvelous work-ing of Satan and that the end is near.—5T 451 (1885).

Rome Will Regain Her Lost Supremacy

As we approach the last crisis it is of vital moment

that harmony and unity exist among the Lord's instrumentalities. The world is filled with storm and war and variance. Yet under one head—the papal power—the people will unite to oppose God in the person of His witnesses. This union is cemented by the great apostate.—7T 182 (1902).

Laws enforcing the observance of Sunday as the Sabbath will bring about a national apostasy from the principles of republicanism upon which the government has been founded. The religion of the papacy will be accepted by the rulers, and the law of God will be made void.—7MR 192 (1906).

A day of great intellectual darkness has been shown to be favorable to the success of popery. It will yet be demonstrated that a day of great intellectual light is equally favorable for its success.—4SP 390 (1884).

In the movements now in progress in the United States to secure for the institutions and usages of the church the support of the state, Protestants are following in the steps of papists. Nay, more, they are opening the door for the papacy to regain in Protestant America the supremacy which she has lost in the Old World.—GC 573 (1911).

A National Sunday Law
Means National Apostasy

To secure popularity and patronage, legislators will yield to the demand for a Sunday law. . . . By the decree enforcing the institution of the papacy in violation of the law of God our nation will disconnect herself fully from righteousness. . . .

As the approach of the Roman armies was a sign to the disciples of the impending destruction of Jerusalem, so may this apostasy be a sign to us that the limit of God's forbearance is reached.—5T 451 (1885).

We must take a firm stand that we will not reverence the first day of the week as the Sabbath, for it is not the day that was blessed and sanctified by Jehovah, and in reverencing Sunday we should place ourselves on the side of the great deceiver. . . .

When the law of God has been made void and apostasy becomes a national sin, the Lord will work in behalf of His people.—3SM 388 (1889).

The people of the United States have been a favored people, but when they restrict religious liberty, surrender Protestantism, and give countenance to popery, the measure of their guilt will be full, and "national apostasy" will be registered in the books of heaven.—RH May 2, 1893.

National Apostasy Will Be Followed by National Ruin

When our nation, in its legislative councils, shall enact laws to bind the consciences of men in regard to their religious privileges, enforcing Sunday observance, and bringing oppressive power to bear against those who keep the seventh-day Sabbath, the law of

God will, to all intents and purposes, be made void in our land, and national apostasy will be followed by national ruin.—7BC 977 (1888).

It is at the time of the national apostasy when, acting on the policy of Satan, the rulers of the land will rank themselves on the side of the man of sin. It is then the measure of guilt is full. The national apostasy is the signal for national ruin.—2SM 373 (1891).

Roman Catholic principles will be taken under the care and protection of the state. This national apostasy will speedily be followed by national ruin. —RH June 15, 1897.

When Protestant churches shall unite with the secular power to sustain a false religion, for opposing which their ancestors endured the fiercest persecution, then will the papal sabbath be enforced by the combined authority of church and state. There will be a national apostasy, which will end only in national ruin.—Ev 235 (1899).

When the state shall use its power to enforce the decrees and sustain the institutions of the church— then will Protestant America have formed an image to the papacy, and there will be a national apostasy which will end only in national ruin.—7BC 976 (1910).

Universal Sunday Legislation

History will be repeated. False religion will be exalted. The first day of the week, a common working day, possessing no sanctity whatever, will be set up as was the image of Babylon. All nations and tongues and peoples will be commanded to worship this spurious sabbath. . . . The decree enforcing the worship of this day is to go forth to all the world.—7BC 976 (1897).

As America, the land of religious liberty, shall unite with the papacy in forcing the conscience and compelling men to honor the false sabbath, the people of every country on the globe will be led to follow her example.—6T 18 (1900).

The Sabbath question is to be the issue in the great final conflict in which all the world will act a part. —6T 352 (1900).

Foreign nations will follow the example of the United States. Though she leads out, yet the same crisis will come upon our people in all parts of the world.—6T 395 (1900).

The substitution of the false for the true is the last act in the drama. When this substitution becomes universal God will reveal Himself. When the laws of men are exalted above the laws of God, when the powers of this earth try to force men to keep the first day of the week, know that the time has come for God to work.—7BC 980 (1901).

The substitution of the laws of men for the law of God, the exaltation, by merely human authority, of Sunday in place of the Bible Sabbath, is the last act in the drama. When this substitution becomes universal God will reveal Himself. He will arise in His majesty to shake terribly the earth.—7T 141 (1902).

The Whole World Will Support Sunday Legislation

The wicked . . . declared that they had the truth, that miracles were among them, that angels from heaven talked with them and walked with them, that great power and signs and wonders were performed among them, and that this was the temporal millennium that they had been expecting so long. The whole world was converted and in harmony with the Sunday law.—3SM 427, 428 (1884).

The whole world is to be stirred with enmity against Seventh-day Adventists because they will not yield homage to the papacy by honoring Sunday, the institution of this antichristian power.—TM 37 (1893).

Those who trample upon God's law make human laws which they will force the people to accept. Men will devise and counsel and plan what they will do. The whole world keeps Sunday, they say, and why should not this people, who are so few in number, do according to the laws of the land?—Ms 163, 1897.

The Controversy Centers in Christendom

The so-called Christian world is to be the theater of great and decisive actions. Men in authority will enact laws controlling the conscience, after the example of the papacy. Babylon will make all nations drink of the wine of the wrath of her fornication. Every nation will be involved. Of this time John the Revelator declares: [Rev. 18:3-7; 17:13, 14, quoted]. "These have one mind." There will be a universal bond of union, one great harmony, a confederacy of Satan's forces. "And shall give their power and strength unto the beast." Thus is manifested the same arbitrary, oppressive power against religious liberty—freedom to worship God according to the dictates of conscience—as was manifested by the papacy, when in the past it persecuted those who dared to refuse to conform with the religious rites and ceremonies of Romanism.—3SM 392 (1891).

In the great conflict between faith and unbelief the whole Christian world will be involved.—RH Feb. 7, 1893.

All Christendom will be divided into two great classes—those who keep the commandments of God and the faith of Jesus, and those who worship the beast and his image and receive his mark.—GC 450 (1911).

As the Sabbath has become the special point of controversy throughout Christendom and religious and secular authorities have combined to enforce the observance of the Sunday, the persistent refusal of a small minority to yield to the popular demand will make them objects of universal execration.—GC 615 (1911).

As the decree issued by the various rulers of Christendom against commandment keepers shall withdraw the protection of government, and abandon them to those who desire their destruction, the people of God will flee from the cities and villages and associate together in companies, dwelling in the most desolate and solitary places.—GC 626 (1911).

Show No Defiance

Those who compose our churches have traits of character that will lead them, if they are not very careful, to feel indignant, because on account of misrepresentation their liberty in regard to working on Sunday is taken away. Do not fly into a passion over this matter but take everything in prayer to God. He alone can restrain the power of rulers. Walk not rashly. Let none boast unwisely of their liberty, using it for a cloak of maliciousness, but as the servants of God, "Honor all men. Love the brotherhood. Fear God. Honor the king" [1 Pet. 2:17].

This advice is to be of real value to all who are to be brought into strait places. Nothing that shows defiance or that could be interpreted as maliciousness must be shown.—2MR 193, 194 (1898).

Refrain From Work on Sunday

In regard to the Southern field,[2] the work there must be done as wisely and carefully as possible, and it must be

---

2. Sunday-law enforcement was especially severe in the southern states in the United States in the 1880s and 1890s. See *American State Papers* (Review and Herald, 1943), pp. 517-562.

done in the manner in which Christ would work. The
people will soon find out what you believe about Sunday
and the Sabbath for they will ask questions. Then you
can tell them, but not in such a manner as to attract
attention to your work. You need not cut short your work
by yourself laboring on Sunday. . . .

Refraining from work on Sunday is not receiving
the mark of the beast. . . . In places where the
opposition is so strong as to arouse persecution, if
work is done on Sunday, let our brethren make that
day an occasion to do genuine missionary work.
—SW 69, 70 (1895).

If they should come here and say "You must close
up your work and your presses on Sunday," I would
not say to you, . . . "Keep your presses going," because
the conflict does not come between you and your
God.—Ms 163, 1898.

We should not feel it enjoined upon us to irritate our
neighbors who idolize Sunday by making determined
efforts to bring labor on that day before them pur-
posely to exhibit an independence. Our sisters need
not select Sunday as the day to exhibit their washing.
—3SM 399 (1889).

Engage in Spiritual Activities on Sunday

I will try to answer your question as to what you
should do in the case of Sunday laws being enforced.

The light given me by the Lord at a time when we
were expecting just such a crisis as you seem to be

approaching, was that when people were moved by a power from beneath to enforce Sunday observance, Seventh-day Adventists were to show their wisdom by refraining from their ordinary work on that day, devoting it to missionary effort.

To defy the Sunday laws will but strengthen in their persecution the religious zealots who are seeking to enforce them. Give them no occasion to call you law-breakers. . . . One does not receive the mark of the beast because he shows that he realizes the wisdom of keeping the peace by refraining from work that gives offense. . . .

Sunday can be used for carrying forward various lines of work that will accomplish much for the Lord. On this day open-air meetings and cottage meetings can be held. House-to-house work can be done. Those who write can devote this day to writing their articles. Whenever it is possible, let religious services be held on Sunday. Make these meetings intensely interesting. Sing genuine revival hymns, and speak with power and assurance of the Saviour's love.—9T 232, 233 (1909).

Take the students out to hold meetings in different places, and to do medical missionary work. They will find the people at home and will have a splendid opportunity to present the truth. This way of spending Sunday is always acceptable to the Lord.—9T 238 (1909).

Beauty of Truth Made
Apparent by Opposition

The zeal of those who obey the Lord will be increased as the world and the church unite in making void the law. Every objection raised against the commandments of God will make way for the advancement of truth and enable its advocates to present its value before men. There is a beauty and force in the truth that nothing can make so apparent as opposition and persecution.—13MR 71, 72 (1896).

This time, when there is such an effort made to enforce the observance of Sunday, is the very opportunity to present to the world the true Sabbath in contrast to the false. The Lord in His providence is far ahead of us. He has permitted this Sunday question to be pressed to the front that the Sabbath of the fourth commandment may be presented before the legislative assemblies. Thus the leading men of the nation may have their attention called to the testimony of God's Word in favor of the true Sabbath.—2MR 197 (1890).

We Ought to Obey God Rather Than Men

The adherents of truth are now called upon to choose between disregarding a plain requirement of God's Word or forfeiting their liberty. If we yield the Word of God and accept human customs and traditions, we may still be permitted to live among men, to buy and sell, and have our rights respected. But if we maintain our loyalty to God it must be at the sacrifice of our rights among men, for the enemies of God's law have leagued together to crush out independent judgment in matters of religious faith and control the consciences of men. . . .

The people of God will recognize human government as an ordinance of divine appointment and will by precept and example teach obedience to it as a sacred duty so long as its authority is exercised within its legitimate sphere. But when its claims conflict with the claims of God we must choose to obey God rather than men. The Word of God must be recognized and obeyed as an authority above that of all human legislation. "Thus saith the Lord" is not to be set aside for a "Thus saith the church or the state." The crown of Christ is to be uplifted above all the diadems of earthly potentates.—HM Nov. 1, 1893.

Satan offers to men the kingdoms of the world if they will yield to him the supremacy. Many do this and sacrifice heaven. It is better to die than to sin; better to want than to defraud; better to hunger than to lie.—4T 495 (1880).

10.

The Little Time of Trouble

A Time of Trouble Before Probation Closes

On page 33 [of *Early Writings*] is given the following: ". . . At the commencement of the time of trouble, we were filled with the Holy Ghost as we went forth and proclaimed the Sabbath more fully."

This view was given in 1847 when there were but very few of the Advent brethren observing the Sabbath, and of these but few supposed that its observance was of sufficient importance to draw a line between the people of God and unbelievers. Now the fulfillment of that view is beginning to be seen. "The commencement of that time of trouble," here mentioned, does not refer to the time when the plagues shall begin to be poured out, but to a short period just before they are poured out, while Christ is in the sanctuary. At that time, while the work of salvation is closing, trouble will be coming on the earth, and the nations will be angry, yet held in check so as not to prevent the work of the third angel.—EW 85, 86 (1854).

The End of Religious
Liberty in the United States

The law of God, through the agency of Satan, is to be made void. In our land of boasted freedom religious liberty will come to an end. The contest will be decided over the Sabbath question, which will agitate the whole world.—Ev 236 (1875).

A great crisis awaits the people of God. Very soon our nation will attempt to enforce upon all the observance of the first day of the week as a sacred day. In doing this they will not scruple to compel men against the voice of their own conscience to observe the day the nation declares to be the Sabbath.—RH Extra, Dec. 11, 1888.

Seventh-day Adventists will fight the battle over the seventh-day Sabbath. The authorities in the United States and in other countries will rise up in their pride and power and make laws to restrict religious liberty.—Ms 78, 1897.

The Protestants of the United States will be foremost in stretching their hands across the gulf to grasp the hand of spiritualism; they will reach over the abyss to clasp hands with the Roman power; and under the influence of this threefold union, this country will follow in the steps of Rome in trampling on the rights of conscience.—GC 588 (1911).

Church and State Oppose God's People

All who will not bow to the decree of the national councils and obey the national laws to exalt the sabbath instituted by the man of sin, to the disregard of God's holy day, will feel, not the oppressive power of popery alone, but of the Protestant world, the image of the beast.—2SM 380 (1886).

Those religious bodies who refuse to hear God's messages of warning will be under strong deception and will unite with the civil power to persecute the saints. The Protestant churches will unite with the papal power in persecuting the commandment-keeping people of God. . . .

This lamb-like power unites with the dragon in making war upon those who keep the commandments of God and have the testimony of Jesus Christ. —14MR 162 (1899).

The church appeals to the strong arm of civil power, and in this work papists and Protestants unite.—GC 607 (1911).

Before the Courts

Those who live during the last days of this earth's history will know what it means to be persecuted for the truth's sake. In the courts injustice will prevail. The judges will refuse to listen to the reasons of those who are loyal to the commandments of God because they know the arguments in favor of the fourth

commandment are unanswerable. They will say, "We
have a law, and by our law he ought to die." God's law
is nothing to them. "Our law" with them is supreme.
Those who respect this human law will be favored, but
those who will not bow to the idol sabbath have no
favors shown them.—ST May 26, 1898.

In cases where we are brought before the courts,
we are to give up our rights, unless it brings us in
collision with God. It is not our rights we are pleading
for, but God's right to our service.—5MR 69 (1895).

Adventists Will Be Treated With Contempt

The same masterful mind that plotted against the
faithful in ages past is still seeking to rid the earth of
those who fear God and obey His law. . . .
Wealth, genius, education, will combine to cover
them with contempt. Persecuting rulers, ministers,
and church members will conspire against them. With
voice and pen, by boasts, threats, and ridicule, they
will seek to overthrow their faith.—5T 450 (1885).

There will come a time when, because of our advo-
cacy of Bible truth, we shall be treated as traitors.
—6T 394 (1900).

Those who honor the Bible Sabbath will be denounced as enemies of law and order, as breaking
down the moral restraints of society, causing anarchy
and corruption, and calling down the judgments of
God upon the earth. Their conscientious scruples will

be pronounced obstinacy, stubbornness, and contempt of authority. They will be accused of disaffection toward the government.—GC 592 (1911).

All who in that evil day would fearlessly serve God according to the dictates of conscience, will need courage, firmness, and a knowledge of God and His Word, for those who are true to God will be persecuted, their motives will be impugned, their best efforts misinterpreted, and their names cast out as evil. —AA 431, 432 (1911).

All Kinds of Persecution

The persecutions of Protestants by Romanism, by which the religion of Jesus Christ was almost annihilated, will be more than rivaled when Protestantism and popery are combined.—3SM 387 (1889).

Satan has a thousand masked batteries which will be opened upon the loyal, commandment-keeping people of God to compel them to violate conscience. —Letter 30a, 1892.

We need not be surprised at anything that may take place now. We need not marvel at any developments of horror. Those who trample under their unholy feet the law of God have the same spirit as had the men who insulted and betrayed Jesus. Without any compunctions of conscience they will do the deeds of their father the devil.—3SM 416 (1897).

Let those who desire to be refreshed in mind and instructed in the truth study the history of the early church during and immediately following the Day of Pentecost. Study carefully in the book of Acts the experiences of Paul and the other apostles, for God's people in our day must pass through similar experiences.—PC 118 (1907).

Every Earthly Support Will Be Cut Off

Hoarded wealth will soon be worthless. When the decree shall go forth that none shall buy or sell except they have the mark of the beast, very much means will be of no avail. God calls for us now to do all in our power to send forth the warning to the world.—RH March 21, 1878.

The time is coming when we cannot sell at any price. The decree will soon go forth prohibiting men to buy or sell of any man save him that hath the mark of the beast. We came near having this realized in California a short time since, but this was only the threatening of the blowing of the four winds. As yet they are held by the four angels. We are not just ready. There is a work yet to be done, and then the angels will be bidden to let go, that the four winds may blow upon the earth.—5T 152 (1882).

In the last great conflict in the controversy with Satan those who are loyal to God will see every earthly support cut off. Because they refuse to break His law in obedience to earthly powers they will be forbidden to buy or sell.—DA 121, 122 (1898).

Satan says . . . "For fear of wanting food and clothing they will join with the world in transgressing God's law. The earth will be wholly under my dominion."—PK 183, 184 (c. 1914).

Some Are Imprisoned for Their Faith

Some will be imprisoned because they refuse to desecrate the Sabbath of the Lord.—PC 118 (1907).

As the defenders of truth refuse to honor the Sunday-sabbath some of them will be thrust into prison, some will be exiled, some will be treated as slaves. To human wisdom all this now seems impossible, but as the restraining Spirit of God shall be withdrawn from men and they shall be under the control of Satan, who hates the divine precepts, there will be strange developments. The heart can be very cruel when God's fear and love are removed.—GC 608 (1911).

If we are called to suffer for Christ's sake, we shall be able to go to prison trusting in Him as a little child trusts in its parents. Now is the time to cultivate faith in God.—OHC 357 (1892).

Many Will Be Put to Death

The best thing for us is to come into close connection with God and, if He would have us be martyrs for the truth's sake, it may be the means of bringing many more into the truth.—3SM 420 (1886).

Many will be imprisoned, many will flee for their lives from cities and towns, and many will be martyrs for Christ's sake in standing in defense of the truth. —3SM 397 (1889).

There is a prospect before us of a continued struggle, at the risk of imprisonment, loss of property and even of life itself, to defend the law of God.—5T 712 (1889).

Men will be required to render obedience to human edicts in violation of the divine law. Those who are true to God will be menaced, denounced, proscribed. They will be "betrayed both by parents, and brethren, and kinsfolks, and friends," even unto death. —PK 588 (c. 1914).

We are not to have the courage and fortitude of martyrs of old until brought into the position they were in. . . . Should there be a return of persecution there would be grace given to arouse every energy of the soul to show a true heroism.—OHC 125 (1889).

The disciples were not endowed with the courage and fortitude of the martyrs until such grace was needed.—DA 354 (1898).

How to Stand Firm Under Persecution

We shall find that we must let loose of all hands except the hand of Jesus Christ. Friends will prove treacherous and will betray us. Relatives, deceived by the enemy, will think they do God service in opposing us and putting forth the utmost efforts to bring us into hard places, hoping we will deny our faith. But we may trust our hand in the hand of Christ amid darkness and peril.—Mar 197 (1889).

The only way in which men will be able to stand firm in the conflict is to be rooted and grounded in Christ. They must receive the truth as it is in Jesus. And it is only as the truth is presented thus that it can meet the wants of the soul. The preaching of Christ crucified, Christ our righteousness, is what satisfies the soul's hunger. When we secure the interest of the people in this great central truth, faith and hope and courage come to the heart.—GCDB Jan. 28, 1893.

Many, because of their faith, will be cut off from house and heritage here, but if they will give their hearts to Christ, receiving the message of His grace, and resting upon their Substitute and Surety, even the Son of God, they may still be filled with joy. —ST June 2, 1898.

Persecution Scatters God's People

As enmity is aroused in various places against those who observe the Sabbath of the Lord, it may become necessary for God's people to move from those places to places where they will not be so bitterly opposed.

God does not require His children to remain where, by the course of wicked men, their influence is made of no effect and their lives endangered. When liberty and life are imperiled it is not merely our privilege, it is our positive duty to go to places where the people are willing to hear the Word of life and where the opportunities for preaching the Word will be more favorable.—Ms 26, 1904.

The time is soon coming when God's people, because of persecution, will be scattered in many countries. Those who have received an all-round education will have the advantage where they are.—5MR 280 (1908).

Persecution Leads to Unity Among God's People

When the storm of persecution really breaks upon us, the true sheep will hear the true Shepherd's voice. Self-denying efforts will be put forth to save the lost, and many who have strayed from the fold will come back to follow the great Shepherd. The people of God will draw together and present to the enemy a united front. In view of the common peril strife for supremacy will cease, there will be no disputing as to who shall be accounted greatest.—6T 401 (1900).

A Crisis Makes God's Interference More Marked

From time to time the Lord has made known His manner of working. He is mindful of what is passing upon the earth. And when a crisis has come, He has revealed Himself and has interposed to hinder the working of Satan's plans. He has often permitted matters with nations, with families, and with individuals to come to a crisis that His interference might become marked. Then He has let the fact be known that there was a God in Israel who would sustain and vindicate His people.

When the defiance of the law of Jehovah shall be almost universal, when His people shall be pressed in affliction by their fellow men, God will interpose. The fervent prayers of His people will be answered, for He loves to have His people seek Him with all their heart and depend upon Him as their Deliverer.—RH June 15, 1897.

For a time the oppressors will be permitted to triumph over those who know God's holy commandments. . . . To the last, God permits Satan to reveal his character as a liar, an accuser, and a murderer. Thus the final triumph of His people is made more marked, more glorious, more full and complete.—3SM 414 (1904).

Affliction Purifies God's People

Soon there is to be trouble all over the world. It becomes everyone to seek to know God. We have no time to delay. . . .

God's love for His church is infinite. His care over His heritage is unceasing. He suffers no affliction to come upon the church but such as is essential for her purification, her present and eternal good. He will purify His church even as He purified the temple at the beginning and close of His ministry on earth. All that He brings upon the church in test and trial comes that His people may gain deeper piety and more strength to carry the triumphs of the cross to all parts of the world.—9T 228 (1909).

Afflictions, crosses, temptations, adversity, and our varied trials are God's workmen to refine us, sanctify us, and fit us for the heavenly garner. —3T 115 (1872).

11.
Satan's Last Day Deceptions

Under the Garb of Christianity

We are approaching the end of this earth's history, and Satan is working as never before. He is striving to act as director of the Christian world. With an intensity that is marvelous he is working with his lying wonders. Satan is represented as walking about as a roaring lion, seeking whom he may devour. He desires to embrace the whole world in his confederacy. Hiding his deformity under the garb of Christianity, he assumes the attributes of a Christian, and claims to be Christ Himself.—8MR 346 (1901).

The Word of God declares that when it suits the enemy's purpose, he will through his agencies manifest so great a power under a pretense of Christianity that, "if it were possible, they shall deceive the very elect" [Matt. 24:24].—Ms 125, 1901.

As the spirits will profess faith in the Bible and manifest respect for the institutions of the church, their work will be accepted as a manifestation of divine power.—GC 588 (1911).

The strongest bulwark of vice in our world is not the iniquitous life of the abandoned sinner or the degraded outcast; it is that life which otherwise appears virtuous, honorable, and noble, but in which one sin is fostered, one vice indulged. . . . Genius, talent, sympathy, even generous and kindly deeds, may thus become decoys of Satan to entice souls over the precipice of ruin.—Ed 150 (1903).

Even in the Adventist Church

We have far more to fear from within than from without. The hindrances to strength and success are far greater from the church itself than from the world. Unbelievers have a right to expect that those who profess to be keeping the commandments of God and the faith of Jesus, will do more than any other class to promote and honor, by their consistent lives, by their godly example and their active influence, the cause which they represent. But how often have the professed advocates of the truth proved the greatest obstacle to its advancement! The unbelief indulged, the doubts expressed, the darkness cherished, encourage the presence of evil angels, and open the way for the accomplishment of Satan's devices.—1SM 122 (1887).

Lying Spirits Contradict the Scriptures

The saints must get a thorough understanding of present truth, which they will be obliged to maintain from the Scriptures. They must understand the state of the dead, for the spirits of devils will yet appear to them, professing to be beloved friends and relatives, who will declare to them that the Sabbath has been changed, also other unscriptural doctrines.—EW 87 (1854).

The apostles, as personated by these lying spirits, are made to contradict what they wrote at the dictation of the Holy Spirit when on earth. They deny the divine origin of the Bible.—GC 557 (1911).

Through the two great errors, the immortality of the soul and Sunday sacredness, Satan will bring the people under his deceptions. While the former lays the foundation of spiritualism, the latter creates a bond of sympathy with Rome.—GC 588 (1911).

Persons will arise pretending to be Christ Himself, and claiming the title and worship which belong to the world's Redeemer. They will perform wonderful miracles of healing, and will profess to have revelations from heaven contradicting the testimony of the Scriptures. . . .

But the people of God will not be misled. The teachings of this false christ are not in accordance with the Scriptures. His blessing is pronounced upon the worshipers of the beast and his image, the very class upon whom the Bible declares that God's unmingled wrath shall be poured out.—GC 624, 625 (1911).

False Revivals

I saw that God has honest children among the nominal Adventists and the fallen churches, and before the plagues shall be poured out, ministers and people will be called out from these churches and will gladly receive the truth. Satan knows this; and before the loud cry of the third angel is given, he raises an excitement in these religious bodies, that those who have rejected the truth may think that God is with them.—EW 261 (1858).

Before the final visitation of God's judgments upon the earth there will be among the people of the Lord such a revival of primitive godliness as has not been witnessed since apostolic times. . . . The enemy of souls desires to hinder this work, and before the time for such a movement shall come, he will endeavor to prevent it by introducing a counterfeit. In those churches which he can bring under his deceptive power, he will make it appear that God's special blessing is poured out; there will be manifest what is thought to be great religious interest. . . .

There is an emotional excitement, a mingling of the true with the false, that is well adapted to mislead. Yet none need be deceived. In the light of God's Word it is not difficult to determine the nature of these movements. Wherever men neglect the testimony of the Bible, turning away from those plain, soul-testing truths which require self-denial and renunciation of the world, there we may be sure that God's blessing is not bestowed.—GC 464 (1911).

Music Is Made a Snare

The things you have described as taking place in Indiana,[1] the Lord has shown me would take place just before the close of probation. Every uncouth thing will be demonstrated. There will be shouting, with drums, music, and dancing. The senses of rational beings will become so confused that they cannot be trusted to make right decisions. . . .

A bedlam of noise shocks the senses and perverts that which if conducted aright might be a blessing. The powers of satanic agencies blend with the din and noise to have a carnival, and this is termed the Holy Spirit's working. . . . Those things which have been in the past will be in the future. Satan will make music a snare by the way in which it is conducted.—2SM 36, 38 (1900).

Let us give no place to strange exercisings, which really take the mind away from the deep movings of the Holy Spirit. God's work is ever characterized by calmness and dignity.—2SM 42 (1908).

False Speaking in Tongues

Fanaticism, false excitement, false talking in tongues, and noisy exercises have been considered gifts which God has placed in the church. Some have been deceived here. The fruits of all this have not been good. "Ye shall know them by their fruits." Fanaticism

1. These comments were made in connection with the "holy flesh" movement at the Indiana camp meeting of 1900. For further details, see *Selected Messages*, book 2, pp. 31-39.

and noise have been considered special evidences of faith. Some are not satisfied with a meeting unless they have a powerful and happy time. They work for this and get up an excitement of feeling. But the influence of such meetings is not beneficial. When the happy flight of feeling is gone they sink lower than before the meeting because their happiness did not come from the right source.

The most profitable meetings for spiritual advancement are those which are characterized with solemnity and deep searching of heart, each seeking to know himself and, earnestly and in deep humility, seeking to learn of Christ.—1T 412 (1864).

Evil Angels Appear as Human Beings

Satan will use every opportunity to seduce men from their allegiance to God. He and the angels who fell with him will appear on the earth as men, seeking to deceive. God's angels also will appear as men, and will use every means in their power to defeat the purposes of the enemy.—8MR 399 (1903).

Evil angels in the form of men will talk with those who know the truth. They will misinterpret and misconstrue the statements of the messengers of God. . . . Have Seventh-day Adventists forgotten the warning given in the sixth chapter of Ephesians? We are engaged in a warfare against the hosts of darkness. Unless we follow our Leader closely, Satan will obtain the victory over us.—3SM 411 (1903).

Evil angels in the form of believers will work in our ranks to bring in a strong spirit of unbelief. Let not even this discourage you, but bring a true heart to the help of the Lord against the powers of satanic agencies. These powers of evil will assemble in our meetings, not to receive a blessing, but to counterwork the influences of the Spirit of God.—2MCP 504, 505 (1909).

Personation of the Dead

It is not difficult for the evil angels to represent both saints and sinners who have died, and make these representations visible to human eyes. These manifestations will be more frequent, and developments of a more startling character will appear as we near the close of time.—Ev 604 (1875).

It is Satan's most successful and fascinating delusion—one calculated to take hold of the sympathies of those who have laid their loved ones in the grave. Evil angels come in the form of those loved ones and relate incidents connected with their lives, and perform acts which they performed while living. In this way they lead persons to believe that their dead friends are angels, hovering over them and communicating with them. These evil angels, who assume to be the deceased friends, are regarded with a certain idolatry, and with many their word has greater weight than the Word of God.—ST Aug. 26, 1889.

He [Satan] has power to bring before men the appearance of their departed friends. The counterfeit is perfect; the familiar look, the words, the tone, are reproduced with marvelous distinctness. . . . Many will be confronted by the spirits of devils personating beloved relatives or friends and declaring the most dangerous heresies. These visitants will appeal to our tenderest sympathies and will work miracles to sustain their pretensions.—GC 552, 560 (1911).

Satan Personates Christ

The enemy is preparing to deceive the whole world by his miracle-working power. He will assume to personate the angels of light, to personate Jesus Christ.—2SM 96 (1894).

If men are so easily misled now, how will they stand when Satan shall personate Christ, and work miracles? Who will be unmoved by his misrepresentations then—professing to be Christ when it is only Satan assuming the person of Christ, and apparently working the works of Christ?—2SM 394 (1897).

Satan will take the field and personate Christ. He will misrepresent, misapply, and pervert everything he possibly can.—TM 411 (1898).

A power from beneath is working to bring about the last great scenes in the drama—Satan coming as Christ, and working with all deceivableness of unrighteousness in those who are binding themselves together in secret societies.—8T 28 (1904).

Satan Resembles Christ in Every Particular

There is a limit beyond which Satan cannot go, and here he calls deception to his aid and counterfeits the work which he has not power actually to perform. In the last days he will appear in such a manner as to make men believe him to be Christ come the second time into the world. He will indeed transform himself into an angel of light. But while he will bear the appearance of Christ in every particular, so far as mere appearance goes, it will deceive none but those who, like Pharaoh, are seeking to resist the truth. —5T 698 (1889).

As the crowning act in the great drama of deception, Satan himself will personate Christ. The church has long professed to look to the Saviour's advent as the consummation of her hopes. Now the great deceiver will make it appear that Christ has come. In different parts of the earth, Satan will manifest himself among men as a majestic being of dazzling brightness, resembling the description of the Son of God given by John in the Revelation (Rev. 1:13-15). The glory that surrounds him is unsurpassed by anything that mortal eyes have yet beheld. The shout of triumph rings out upon the air: "Christ has come! Christ has come!"

The people prostrate themselves in adoration before him, while he lifts up his hands and pronounces a blessing upon them, as Christ blessed His disciples when He was upon the earth. His voice is soft and subdued, yet full of melody. In gentle, compassionate tones he presents some of the same gracious, heavenly truths which the Saviour uttered; he heals the diseases of the people, and then, in his assumed character of Christ, he claims to have changed the Sabbath to Sunday, and commands all to hallow the day which he has blessed.—GC 624 (1911).

Satan Pretends to Answer the Saints' Prayers

Satan sees that he is about to lose his case. He cannot sweep in the whole world. He makes one last desperate effort to overcome the faithful by deception. He does this in personating Christ. He clothes himself with the garments of royalty which have been accurately described in the vision of John. He has power to do this. He will appear to his deluded followers, the Christian world who received not the love of the truth but had pleasure in unrighteousness (transgression of the law), as Christ coming the second time.

He proclaims himself Christ, and he is believed to be Christ, a beautiful, majestic being clothed with majesty and, with soft voice and pleasant words, with glory unsurpassed by anything their mortal eyes had yet beheld. Then his deceived, deluded followers set up a shout of victory, "Christ has come the second time! Christ has come! He has lifted up His hands just as He did when He was upon the earth, and blessed us.". . .

The saints look on with amazement. Will they also be deceived? Will they worship Satan? Angels of God are about them. A clear, firm, musical voice is heard, "Look up."

There was one object before the praying ones—the final and eternal salvation of their souls. This object was before them constantly—that immortal life was promised to those who endure unto the end. Oh, how earnest and fervent had been their desires. The judgment and eternity were in view. Their eyes by faith were fixed on the blazing throne, before which the white-robed ones were to stand. This restrained them from the indulgence of sin. . . .

One effort more, and then Satan's last device is employed. He hears the unceasing cry for Christ to come, for Christ to deliver them. This last strategy is to personate Christ, and make them think their prayers are answered.—Ms 16, 1884.

How the Counterfeit
Differs From the Genuine

Satan is not permitted to counterfeit the manner of Christ's advent.—GC 625 (1911).

Satan . . . will come personating Jesus Christ, working mighty miracles; and men will fall down and worship him as Jesus Christ. We shall be commanded to worship this being, whom the world will glorify as Christ. What shall we do? Tell them that Christ has warned us against just such a foe, who is man's worst enemy, yet who claims to be God, and that when Christ shall make His appearance it will be with power and great glory, accompanied by ten thousand times ten thousand angels and thousands of thousands, and that when He shall come we shall know His voice.—6BC 1106 (1888).

Satan is striving to gain every advantage. . . . Disguised as an angel of light, he will walk the earth as a wonder-worker. In beautiful language he will present lofty sentiments; good words will be spoken by him and good deeds performed. Christ will be personified. But on one point there will be a marked distinction—Satan will turn the people from the law of God. Notwithstanding this, so well will he counterfeit righteousness that, if it were possible, he would deceive the very elect. Crowned heads, presidents, rulers in high places, will bow to his false theories. —FE 471, 472 (1897).

Miracles Will Be Performed

The sick will be healed before us. Miracles will be performed in our sight. Are we prepared for the trial which awaits us when the lying wonders of Satan shall be more fully exhibited?—1T 302 (1862).

Men under the influence of evil spirits will work miracles. They will make people sick by casting their spell upon them, and will then remove the spell, leading others to say that those who were sick have been miraculously healed. This Satan has done again and again.—2SM 53 (1903).

Wonderful scenes, with which Satan will be closely connected, will soon take place. God's Word declares that Satan will work miracles. He will make people sick, and then will suddenly remove from them his satanic power. They will then be regarded as healed.

These works of apparent healing will bring Seventh-day Adventists to the test.—2SM 53 (1904).

Satan can, through a species of deceptions, perform wonders that will appear to be genuine miracles. It was this he hoped to make a test question with the Israelites at the time of their deliverance from Egypt. —2SM 52 (1907).

Fire From Heaven

We must not trust the claims of men. They may, as Christ represents, profess to work miracles in healing the sick. Is this marvelous, when just behind them stands the great deceiver, the miracle worker who will yet bring down fire from heaven in the sight of men? —2SM 49 (1887).

It is the lying wonders of the devil that will take the world captive, and he will cause fire to come down from heaven in the sight of men. He is to work miracles, and this wonderful, miracle-working power is to sweep in the whole world.—2SM 51 (1890).

Satan will come in to deceive if possible the very elect. He claims to be Christ, and he is coming in, pretending to be the great medical missionary. He will cause fire to come down from heaven in the sight of men to prove that he is God.—MM 87, 88 (1903).

It is stated in the Word that the enemy will work through his agents who have departed from the faith, and they will seemingly work miracles, even to the bringing down of fire out of heaven in the sight of men.—2SM 54 (1907).

"He doeth great wonders, so that he maketh fire come down from heaven on the earth in the sight of men, and deceiveth them that dwell on the earth by the means of those miracles which he had power to do" (Rev. 13:13, 14). No mere impostures are here foretold. Men are deceived by the miracles which Satan's agents have power to do, not which they pretend to do.—GC 553 (1911).

Satan Will Be Deified

In this age antichrist will appear as the true Christ, and then the law of God will be fully made void in the nations of our world. Rebellion against God's holy law will be fully ripe. But the true leader of all this rebellion is Satan clothed as an angel of light. Men will be deceived and will exalt him to the place of God, and deify him. But Omnipotence will interpose, and to the apostate churches that unite in the exaltation of Satan, the sentence will go forth, "Therefore shall her plagues come in one day, death, and mourning, and famine; and she shall be utterly burned with fire: for strong is the Lord God who judgeth her" [Rev. 18:8].—TM 62 (1893).

As the second appearing of our Lord Jesus Christ draws near, satanic agencies are moved from beneath. Satan will not only appear as a human being, but he will personate Jesus Christ, and the world that has rejected the truth will receive him as the Lord of lords and King of kings.—5BC 1105, 1106 (1900).

Miracles Prove Nothing

Go to God for yourselves, pray for divine enlightenment, that you may know that you do know what is truth, that when the wonderful miracle-working power shall be displayed, and the enemy shall come as an angel of light, you may distinguish between the genuine work of God and the imitative work of the powers of darkness.—3SM 389 (1888).

The way in which Christ worked was to preach the Word, and to relieve suffering by miraculous works of healing. But I am instructed that we cannot now work in this way,[2] for Satan will exercise his power by working miracles. God's servants today could not work by means of miracles, because spurious works of healing, claiming to be divine, will be wrought.—2SM 54 (1904).

God's people will not find their safety in working miracles, for Satan will counterfeit the miracles that will be wrought.—9T 16 (1909).

Miracles Cannot Supersede the Bible

If those through whom cures are performed are disposed, on account of these manifestations, to ex-

2. Miracles will accompany the ministry of God's people under the Loud Cry (see chapter 14), but they will not have the significance they did in Christ's day. The performing of miracles will no longer be a proof of divine endorsement.

cuse their neglect of the law of God and continue in disobedience, though they have power to any and every extent, it does not follow that they have the great power of God. On the contrary, it is the miracle-working power of the great deceiver.—2SM 50, 51 (1885).

The Bible will never be superseded by miraculous manifestations. The truth must be studied, it must be searched for as hidden treasure. Wonderful illuminations will not be given aside from the Word or to take the place of it. Cling to the Word, receive the engrafted Word which will make men wise unto salvation. —2SM 48 (1894).

The last great delusion is soon to open before us. Antichrist is to perform his marvelous works in our sight. So closely will the counterfeit resemble the true that it will be impossible to distinguish between them except by the Holy Scriptures. By their testimony every statement and every miracle must be tested. —GC 593 (1911).

The Deception Is Almost Universal

There is now need of earnest, working men and women who will seek for the salvation of souls, for Satan as a powerful general has taken the field, and in this last remnant of time he is working through all conceivable methods to close the door against light that God would have come to His people. He is sweeping the whole world into his ranks, and the few who are faithful to God's requirements are the only ones who can ever withstand him, and even these he is trying to overcome.—3SM 389 (1889).

The forms of the dead will appear, through the cunning device of Satan, and many will link up with the one who loveth and maketh a lie. I warn our people that right among us some will turn away from the faith and give heed to seducing spirits and doctrines of devils, and by them the truth will be evil spoken of.

A marvelous work shall take place. Ministers, lawyers, doctors, who have permitted these false-hoods to overmaster their spirit of discernment, will be themselves deceivers, united with the deceived. A spiritual drunkenness will take possession of them. —UL 317 (1905).

12.

The Shaking

Church Membership No Guarantee of Salvation

It is a solemn statement that I make to the church, that not one in twenty whose names are registered upon the church books are prepared to close their earthly history, and would be as verily without God and without hope in the world as the common sinner.—ChS 41 (1893).

Those who have had opportunities to hear and receive the truth and who have united with the Seventh-day Adventist church, calling themselves the commandment-keeping people of God, and yet possess no more vitality and consecration to God than do the nominal churches, will receive of the plagues of God just as verily as the churches who oppose the law of God.—19MR 176 (1898).

The Chaff Separated From the Wheat

Divisions will come in the church. Two parties will be developed. The wheat and tares grow up together for the harvest.—2SM 114 (1896).

There will be a shaking of the sieve. The chaff must in time be separated from the wheat. Because iniquity abounds, the love of many waxes cold. It is the very time when the genuine will be the strongest.—Letter 46, 1887.

The history of the rebellion of Dathan and Abiram is being repeated, and will be repeated till the close of time. Who will be on the Lord's side? Who will be deceived, and in their turn become deceivers?—Letter 15, 1892.

The Lord is soon to come. There must be a refining, winnowing process in every church, for there are among us wicked men who do not love the truth or honor God.—RH March 19, 1895.

We are in the shaking time, the time when everything that can be shaken will be shaken. The Lord will not excuse those who know the truth if they do not in word and deed obey His commands.—6T 332 (1900).

Persecution Cleanses the Church

Prosperity multiplies a mass of professors. Adversity purges them out of the church.—4T 89 (1876).

The time is not far distant when the test will come to every soul. The mark of the beast will be urged upon us. Those who have step by step yielded to worldly demands and conformed to worldly customs will not find it a hard matter to yield to the powers that be, rather than subject themselves to derision, insult, threatened imprisonment, and death. The contest is between the commandments of God and the commandments of men. In this time the gold will be separated from the dross in the church.—5T 81 (1882).

In the absence of the persecution there have drifted into our ranks men who appear sound and their Christianity unquestionable, but who, if persecution should arise, would go out from us.—Ev 360 (1890).

When the law of God is made void the church will be sifted by fiery trials, and a larger proportion than we now anticipate will give heed to seducing spirits and doctrines of devils.—2SM 368 (1891).

Superficial Believers Will Renounce the Faith

The work which the church has failed to do in a time of peace and prosperity she will have to do in a terrible crisis under most discouraging, forbidding circumstances. The warnings that worldly conformity has silenced or withheld must be given under the fiercest opposition from enemies of the faith. And at that time the superficial, conservative[1] class, whose influence has steadily retarded the progress of the work, will renounce the faith.—5T 463 (1885).

If Satan sees that the Lord is blessing His people and preparing them to discern his delusions, he will

---

1. Ellen White is not here distinguishing theological conservatives from their liberal counterparts; she is describing those who put "worldly conformity" first and God's cause second.

work with his master power to bring in fanaticism on the one hand and cold formalism on the other, that he may gather in a harvest of souls.—2SM 19 (1890).

Those who have had privileges and opportunities to become intelligent in regard to the truth and yet who continue to counterwork the work God would have accomplished will be purged out, for God accepts the service of no man whose interest is divided.—Ms 64, 1898.

As trials thicken around us, both separation and unity will be seen in our ranks. Some who are now ready to take up weapons of warfare will in times of real peril make it manifest that they have not built upon the solid rock; they will yield to temptation. Those who have had great light and precious privileges but have not improved them will, under one pretext or another, go out from us.—6T 400 (1900).

The Straight Testimony Produces a Shaking

I asked the meaning of the shaking I had seen, and was shown that it would be caused by the straight testimony called forth by the counsel of the True Witness to the Laodiceans. This will have its effect upon the heart of the receiver, and will lead him to exalt the standard and pour forth the straight truth. Some will not bear this straight testimony. They will rise up against it, and this will cause a shaking among God's people.—1T 181 (1857).

There are those among us who will make confessions, as did Achan, too late to save themselves.

... They are not in harmony with right. They despise the straight testimony that reaches the heart, and would rejoice to see everyone silenced who gives reproof.—3T 272 (1873).

The Lord calls for a renewal of the straight testimony borne in years past. He calls for a renewal of spiritual life. The spiritual energies of His people have long been torpid, but there is to be a resurrection from apparent death. By prayer and confession of sin we must clear the King's highway.—8T 297 (1904).

Unjust Criticism Causes Loss of Souls

Even in our day there have been and will continue to be entire families who have once rejoiced in the truth, but who will lose faith because of calumnies and falsehoods brought to them in regard to those whom they have loved and with whom they have had sweet counsel. They opened their hearts to the sowing of tares, the tares sprang up among the wheat, they strengthened, the crop of wheat became less and less, and the precious truth lost its power to them. —TM 411 (1898).

False Doctrines Draw Some Away

Science, so-called, and religion will be placed in opposition to each other because finite men do not comprehend the power and greatness of God. These words of Holy Writ were presented to me, "Of your own selves shall men arise, speaking perverse things, to draw away disciples after them" [Acts 20:30]. This will surely be seen among the people of God.—Ev 593 (1890).

When the shaking comes, by the introduction of false theories, these surface readers, anchored no-where, are like shifting sand. They slide into any position to suit the tenor of their feelings of bitter-ness.—TM 112 (1897).

Not having received the love of the truth, they will be taken in the delusions of the enemy; they will give heed to seducing spirits and doctrines of devils and will depart from the faith.—6T 401 (1900).

The enemy will bring in false theories, such as the doctrine that there is no sanctuary. This is one of the points on which there will be a departing from the faith.—Ev 224 (1905).

Rejection of the
Testimonies Results in Apostasy

One thing is certain: Those Seventh-day Adventists who take their stand under Satan's banner will first give up their faith in the warnings and reproofs contained in the Testimonies of God's Spirit.—3SM 84 (1903).

The very last deception of Satan will be to make of none effect the testimony of the Spirit of God. "Where there is no vision, the people perish" (Prov. 29:18). Satan will work ingeniously, in different ways and through different agencies, to unsettle the confidence of God's remnant people in the true testimony.—1 SM 48 (1890).

The enemy has made his masterly efforts to unsettle the faith of our own people in the *Testimonies*. . . . This is just as Satan designed it should be, and those who have been preparing the way for the people to pay no heed to the warnings and reproofs of the *Testimonies* of the Spirit of God will see that a tide of errors of all kinds will spring into life.—3SM 83 (1890).

It is Satan's plan to weaken the faith of God's people in the *Testimonies*. Next follows skepticism in regard to the vital points of our faith, the pillars of our position, then doubt as to the Holy Scriptures, and then the downward march to perdition. When the *Testimonies*, which were once believed, are doubted and given up, Satan knows the deceived ones will not stop at this; and he redoubles his efforts till he launches them into open rebellion, which becomes incurable and ends in destruction.—4T 211.

Defections Among Church Leaders

Many a star that we have admired for its brilliance will then go out in darkness.—PK 188 (c. 1914).

Men whom He has greatly honored will, in the closing scenes of this earth's history, pattern after ancient Israel. . . . A departure from the great principles Christ has laid down in His teachings, a working out of human projects, using the Scriptures to justify a wrong course of action under the perverse working of Lucifer, will confirm men in misunderstanding, and the truth that they need to keep them from wrong practices will leak out of the soul like water from a leaky vessel.—13MR 379, 381 (1904).

Many will show that they are not one with Christ, that they are not dead to the world, that they may live with Him; and frequent will be the apostasies of men who have occupied responsible positions.—RH Sept. 11, 1888.

Unsanctified Ministers Will Be Weeded Out

The great issue so near at hand [enforcement of Sunday laws] will weed out those whom God has not appointed and He will have a pure, true, sanctified ministry prepared for the latter rain.—3SM 385 (1886).

Many will stand in our pulpits with the torch of false prophecy in their hands, kindled from the hellish torch of Satan. . . .

Some will go out from among us who will bear the ark no longer. But these can not make walls to obstruct the truth; for it will go onward and upward to the end.—TM 409, 411 (1898).

Ministers and doctors may depart from the faith, as the Word declares they will, and as the messages that God has given His servant declare they will. —7MR 192 (1906).

The Church May Appear as About to Fall

The shaking of God blows away multitudes like dry leaves.—4T 89 (1876).

Chaff like a cloud will be borne away on the wind, even from places where we see only floors of rich wheat.—5T 81 (1882).

Soon God's people will be tested by fiery trials, and the great proportion of those who now appear to be genuine and true will prove to be base metal. . . .

When the religion of Christ is most held in contempt, when His law is most despised, then should our zeal be the warmest and our courage and firmness the most unflinching. To stand in defense of truth and righteousness when the majority forsake us, to fight the battles of the Lord when champions are few—this will be our test. At this time we must gather warmth from the coldness of others, courage from their cowardice, and loyalty from their treason.—5T 136 (1882).

The church may appear as about to fall, but it does not fall. It remains, while the sinners in Zion will be sifted out—the chaff separated from the precious wheat. This is a terrible ordeal, but nevertheless it must take place.—2SM 380 (1886).

As the storm approaches, a large class who have professed faith in the third angel's message, but have not been sanctified through obedience to the truth, abandon their position and join the ranks of the opposition.—GC 608 (1911).

God's Faithful Will Be Revealed

The Lord has faithful servants who in the shaking, testing time will be disclosed to view. There are precious ones now hidden who have not bowed the knee to Baal. They have not had the light which has been shining in a concentrated blaze upon you. But it may be under a rough and uninviting exterior the pure brightness of a genuine Christian character will be revealed. In the daytime we look toward heaven but do not see the stars. They are there, fixed in the firmament, but the eye cannot distinguish them. In the night we behold their genuine luster.—5T 80, 81 (1882).

On every occasion that persecution takes place, the witnesses make decisions, either for Christ or against Him. Those who show sympathy for the men wrongly condemned, who are not bitter against them, show their attachment for Christ.—ST Feb. 20, 1901.

Let opposition arise, let bigotry and intolerance again bear sway, let persecution be kindled, and the half-hearted and hypocritical will waver and yield the faith; but the true Christian will stand firm as a rock, his faith stronger, his hope brighter than in days of prosperity.—GC 602 (1911).

New Converts Will Take
the Places of Those Who Leave

Some had been shaken out and left by the way. The careless and indifferent, who did not join with those who prized victory and salvation enough to perseveringly plead and agonize for it, did not obtain it, and they were left behind in darkness, and their places were immediately filled by others taking hold of the truth and coming into the ranks.—EW 271 (1858).

The broken ranks will be filled up by those represented by Christ as coming in at the eleventh hour. There are many with whom the Spirit of God is striving. The time of God's destructive judgments is the time of mercy for those who [now] have no opportunity to learn what is truth. Tenderly will the Lord look upon them. His heart of mercy is touched, His hand is still stretched out to save, while the door is closed to those who would not enter. Large numbers will be admitted who in these last days hear the truth for the first time.—Letter 103, 1903.

Standard after standard was left to trail in the dust as company after company from the Lord's army joined the foe and tribe after tribe from the ranks of the enemy united with the commandment-keeping people of God.—8T 41 (1904).

13.

The Latter Rain

The Work of the Spirit Likened to Rain

"He will cause to come down for you the rain, the former rain, and the latter rain." In the East the former rain falls at the sowing time. It is necessary in order that the seed may germinate. Under the influence of the fertilizing showers the tender shoot springs up. The latter rain, falling near the close of the season, ripens the grain and prepares it for the sickle. The Lord employs these operations of nature to represent the work of the Holy Spirit.[1]

As the dew and the rain are given first to cause the seed to germinate, and then to ripen the harvest, so the Holy Spirit is given to carry forward, from one stage to another, the process of spiritual growth. The ripening of the grain represents the completion of the work of God's grace in the soul. By the power of the Holy Spirit the moral image of God is to be perfected in the character. We are to be wholly transformed into the likeness of Christ.

The latter rain, ripening earth's harvest, represents the spiritual grace that prepares the church for the coming of the Son of man. But unless the former

---

1. See Zechariah 10:1; Hosea 6:3; Joel 2:23, 28.

rain has fallen, there will be no life; the green blade will not spring up. Unless the early showers have done their work, the latter rain can bring no seed to perfection.—TM 506 (1897).

A. *The Historical Application To the Church as a Whole*

The Early Rain Came in A.D. 31 at Pentecost

In obedience to Christ's command, they [the disciples] waited in Jerusalem for the promise of the Father—the outpouring of the Spirit. They did not wait in idleness. The record says that they were "continually in the temple, praising and blessing God" (Luke 24:53. . . .

As the disciples waited for the fulfillment of the promise, they humbled their hearts in true repentance and confessed their unbelief. . . . The disciples prayed with intense earnestness for a fitness to meet men and in their daily intercourse to speak words that would lead sinners to Christ. Putting away all differences, all desire for the supremacy, they came close together in Christian fellowship.—AA 35-37 (1911).

It was after the disciples had come into perfect unity, when they were no longer striving for the highest place, that the Spirit was poured out.—8T 20 (1904).

The outpouring of the Spirit in the days of the apostles was the beginning of the early, or former, rain, and glorious was the result. To the end of time the presence of the Spirit is to abide with the true church.—AA 54, 55 (1911).

Consequences of the Early Rain at Pentecost

Under the influence of the Spirit, words of penitence and confession mingled with songs of praise for sins forgiven. . . . Thousands were converted in a day. . . .

The Holy Spirit . . . enabled them to speak with fluency languages with which they had heretofore been unacquainted. . . . The Holy Spirit did for them that which they could not have accomplished for themselves in a lifetime.—AA 38-40 (1911).

Their hearts were surcharged with a benevolence so full, so deep, so far-reaching, that it impelled them to go to the ends of the earth, testifying to the power of Christ.—AA 46 (1911).

What was the result of the outpouring of the Spirit on the Day of Pentecost? The glad tidings of a risen Saviour were carried to the uttermost parts of the inhabited world. . . . The church beheld converts flocking to her from all directions. Backsliders were reconverted. . . . The ambition of the believers was to reveal the likeness of Christ's character and to labor for the enlargement of His kingdom.—AA 48 (1911).

The Promise of the Latter Rain

The outpouring of the Spirit in the days of the apostles was "the former rain," and glorious was the

result. But the latter rain will be more abundant.
—8T 21 (1904).

Near the close of earth's harvest, a special bestowal
of spiritual grace is promised to prepare the church for
the coming of the Son of man. This outpouring of the
Spirit is likened to the falling of the latter rain.
—AA 55 (1911).

Before the final visitation of God's judgments upon
the earth there will be among the people of the Lord such
a revival of primitive godliness as has not been witnessed since apostolic times. The Spirit and power of God
will be poured out upon His children.—GC 464 (1911).

The work will be similar to that of the Day of
Pentecost. As the "former rain" was given, in the
outpouring of the Holy Spirit at the opening of the
gospel, to cause the upspringing of the precious seed,
so the "latter rain" will be given at its close for the
ripening of the harvest.—GC 611 (1911).

The Latter Rain Will Produce the Loud Cry

At that time the "latter rain," or refreshing from the
presence of the Lord, will come, to give power to the
loud voice of the third angel, and prepare the saints to
stand in the period when the seven last plagues shall
be poured out.—EW 86 (1854).

I heard those clothed with the armor speak forth the
truth with great power. It had effect. . . . I asked what

had made this great change. An angel answered, "It is the latter rain, the refreshing from the presence of the Lord, the loud cry of the third angel."—EW 271 (1858).

B. The Personal Application
To Individual Christians

The Early Rain Produces Conversion; The Latter Rain Develops a Christlike Character

At no point in our experience can we dispense with the assistance of that which enables us to make the first start. The blessings received under the former rain are needful to us to the end. . . . As we seek God for the Holy Spirit, it will work in us meekness, humbleness of mind, a conscious dependence upon God for the perfecting latter rain.—TM 507, 509 (1897).

The Holy Spirit seeks to abide in each soul. If it is welcomed as an honored guest, those who receive it will be made complete in Christ. The good work begun will be finished; the holy thoughts, heavenly affections, and Christlike actions will take the place of impure thoughts, perverse sentiments, and rebellious acts.—CH 561 (1896).

We may have had a measure of the Spirit of God, but by prayer and faith we are continually to seek more of the Spirit. It will never do to cease our efforts. If we do not progress, if we do not place ourselves in an attitude to receive both the former and the latter rain, we shall lose our souls, and the responsibility will lie at our own door. . . .

The convocations of the church, as in camp meetings, the assemblies of the home church, and all occasions where there is personal labor for souls, are God's appointed opportunities for giving the early and the latter rain.—TM 508 (1897).

When the way is prepared for the Spirit of God, the blessing will come. Satan can no more hinder a shower of blessing from descending upon God's people than he can close the windows of heaven that rain cannot come upon the earth.—1SM 124 (1887).

We Should Pray Earnestly for the Descent of the Holy Spirit

We should pray as earnestly for the descent of the Holy Spirit as the disciples prayed on the Day of Pentecost. If they needed it at that time, we need it more today.—5T 158 (1882).

The descent of the Holy Spirit upon the church is looked forward to as in the future, but it is the privilege of the church to have it now. Seek for it, pray for it, believe for it. We must have it, and Heaven is waiting to bestow it.—Ev 701 (1895).

The measure of the Holy Spirit we receive will be proportioned to the measure of our desire and the faith exercised for it, and the use we shall make of the light and knowledge that shall be given to us.—RH May 5, 1896.

We are not willing enough to trouble the Lord with our petitions, and to ask Him for the gift of the Holy

Spirit. The Lord wants us to trouble Him in this matter. He wants us to press our petitions to the throne.—FE 537 (1909).

We Must Humble Our
Hearts in True Repentance

A revival of true godliness among us is the greatest and most urgent of all our needs. To seek this should be our first work. There must be earnest effort to obtain the blessing of the Lord, not because God is not willing to bestow His blessing upon us, but because we are unprepared to receive it. Our heavenly Father is more willing to give His Holy Spirit to them that ask Him, than are earthly parents to give good gifts to their children. But it is our work, by confession, humiliation, repentance, and earnest prayer, to fulfill the conditions upon which God has promised to grant us His blessing. A revival need be expected only in answer to prayer.—1SM 121 (1887).

I tell you that there must be a thorough revival among us. There must be a converted ministry. There must be confessions, repentance, and conversions. Many who are preaching the Word need the transforming grace of Christ in their hearts. They should let nothing stand in the way of their making thorough work before it shall be forever too late.—Letter 51, 1886.

Reformation Must Accompany Revival

A revival and a reformation must take place, under the ministration of the Holy Spirit. Revival and reformation are two different things. Revival signifies a renewal of spiritual life, a quickening of the powers of mind and heart, a resurrection from spiritual death. Reformation signifies a reorganization, a change in ideas and theories, habits and practices. Reformation will not bring forth the good fruit of righteousness unless it is connected with the revival of the Spirit. Revival and reformation are to do their appointed work, and in doing this work they must blend.—RH Feb. 25, 1902.

We Must Put Away All Strife and Dissension

When the laborers have an abiding Christ in their own souls, when all selfishness is dead, when there is no rivalry, no strife for the supremacy, when oneness exists, when they sanctify themselves, so that love for one another is seen and felt, then the showers of the grace of the Holy Spirit will just as surely come upon them as that God's promise will never fail in one jot or tittle. But when the work of others is discounted, that the workers may show their own superiority, they prove that their own work does not bear the signature it should. God cannot bless them.—1SM 175 (1896).

If we stand in the great day of the Lord with Christ as our refuge, our high tower, we must put away all envy, all strife for the supremacy. We must utterly destroy the roots of these unholy things, that they may not again spring up into life. We must place ourselves wholly on the side of the Lord.—TDG 258 (1903).

Let Christians put away all dissension and give themselves to God for the saving of the lost. Let them ask in faith for the promised blessing, and it will come.—8T 21 (1904).

Love One Another

Christianity is the revealing of the tenderest affection for one another. . . . Christ is to receive supreme love from the beings He has created. And He requires also that man shall cherish a sacred regard for his fellow beings. Every soul saved will be saved through love, which begins with God. True conversion is a change from selfishness to sanctified affection for God and for one another.—1SM 114, 115 (1901).

The attributes which God prizes most are charity and purity. These attributes should be cherished by every Christian.—5T 85 (1882).

The strongest argument in favor of the gospel is a loving and lovable Christian.—MH 470 (1905).

Total Surrender Required

God will accept nothing less than unreserved surrender. Half-hearted, sinful Christians can never enter heaven. There they would find no happiness, for they know nothing of the high, holy principles that govern the members of the royal family. The true Christian keeps the windows of the soul open heavenward. He lives in fellowship with Christ. His will is conformed to the will of Christ. His highest desire is to become more and more Christlike.—RH May 16, 1907.

We cannot use the Holy Spirit. The Spirit is to use us. Through the Spirit God works in His people "to will and to do of His good pleasure" (Phil. 2:13). But many will not submit to this. They want to manage themselves. This is why they do not receive the heavenly gift. Only to those who wait humbly upon God, who watch for His guidance and grace, is the Spirit given.—DA 672 (1898).

Clearing the Way for the Latter Rain

I saw that none could share the "refreshing" unless they obtain the victory over every besetment, over pride, selfishness, love of the world, and over every wrong word and action. We should therefore be drawing nearer and nearer to the Lord and be earnestly seeking that preparation necessary to enable us to stand in the battle in the day of the Lord.—EW 71 (1851).

It is left with us to remedy the defects in our characters, to cleanse the soul temple of every defilement. Then the latter rain will fall upon us as the early rain fell upon the disciples on the Day of Pentecost. —5T 214 (1882).

There is nothing that Satan fears so much as that the people of God shall clear the way by removing every hindrance, so that the Lord can pour out His Spirit upon a languishing church. . . . Every temptation, every opposing influence, whether open or secret, may be successfully resisted, "not by might, nor by power, but by my Spirit, saith the Lord of hosts" (Zech. 4:6).—1SM 124 (1887).

The latter rain will come, and the blessing of God will fill every soul that is purified from every defilement. It is our work today to yield our souls to Christ, that we may be fitted for the time of refreshing from the presence of the Lord—fitted for the baptism of the Holy Spirit.—1SM 191 (1892).

Become Active Laborers in Christ's Service

When the churches become living, working churches, the Holy Spirit will be given in answer to their sincere request. . . . Then the windows of heaven will be open for the showers of the latter rain. —RH Feb. 25, 1890.

The great outpouring of the Spirit of God, which lightens the whole earth with His glory, will not come until we have an enlightened people, that know by experience what it means to be laborers together with God. When we have entire, wholehearted consecration to the service of Christ, God will recognize the fact by an outpouring of His Spirit without measure; but this will not be while the largest portion of the church are not laborers together with God.—ChS 253 (1896).

When the reproach of indolence and slothfulness shall have been wiped away from the church, the Spirit of the Lord will be graciously manifested. Divine power will be revealed. The church will see the providential working of the Lord of hosts.—9T 46 (1909).

"Keep the Vessel Clean and Right Side Up"

We need not worry about the latter rain. All we have to do is to keep the vessel clean and right side up and prepared for the reception of the heavenly rain, and keep praying, "Let the latter rain come into my vessel. Let the light of the glorious angel which unites with the third angel shine upon me; give me a part in the work; let me sound the proclamation; let me be a colaborer with Jesus Christ." Thus seeking God, let me tell you, He is fitting you up all the time, giving you His grace.—UL 283 (1891).

The answer may come with sudden velocity and overpowering might, or it may be delayed for days and weeks, and our faith receive a trial. But God knows how and when to answer our prayer. It is *our* part of the work to put ourselves in connection with the divine channel. God is responsible for *His* part of the work. He is faithful who hath promised. The great and important matter with us is to be of one heart and mind, putting aside all envy and malice and, as humble supplicants, to watch and wait. Jesus, our Representative and Head, is ready to do for us what He did for the praying, watching ones on the Day of Pentecost.—3SP 272 (1878).

I have no specific time of which to speak when the outpouring of the Holy Spirit will take place—when the mighty angel will come down from heaven and unite with the third angel in closing up the work for this world. My message is that our only safety is in being ready for the heavenly refreshing, having our lamps trimmed and burning.—1SM 192 (1892).

Not All Will Receive the Latter Rain

I was shown that if God's people make no efforts on their part, but wait for the refreshing to come upon them and remove their wrongs and correct their errors; if they depend upon that to cleanse them from filthiness of the flesh and spirit, and fit them to engage in the loud cry of the third angel, they will be found wanting.—1T 619 (1867).

Are we hoping to see the whole church revived? That time will never come. There are persons in the church who are not converted, and who will not unite in earnest, prevailing prayer. We must enter upon the work individually. We must pray more, and talk less.—1SM 122 (1887).

We may be sure that when the Holy Spirit is poured out, those who did not receive and appreciate the early rain will not see or understand the value of the latter rain.—TM 399 (1896).

Only those who are living up to the light they have will receive greater light. Unless we are daily advancing in the exemplification of the active Christian virtues, we shall not recognize the manifestations of the Holy Spirit in the latter rain. It may be falling on hearts all around us, but we shall not discern or receive it.—TM 507 (1897).

Those who make no decided effort, but simply wait for the Holy Spirit to compel them to action, will perish in darkness. You are not to sit still and do nothing in the work of God.—ChS 228 (1903).

14.

The Loud Cry

God Has Jewels in All Churches

God has jewels in all the churches, and it is not for us to make sweeping denunciation of the professed religious world.—4BC 1184 (1893).

The Lord has His representatives in all the churches. These persons have not had the special testing truths for these last days presented to them under circumstances that brought conviction to heart and mind; therefore they have not, by rejecting light, severed their connection with God.—6T 70, 71 (1900).

Among the Catholics there are many who are most conscientious Christians and who walk in all the light that shines upon them, and God will work in their behalf.—9T 243 (1909).

In the eighteenth chapter of the Revelation the people of God are called upon to come out of Babylon. According to this scripture, many of God's people must still be in Babylon. And in what religious bodies are the greater part of the followers of Christ now to be found? Without doubt, in the various churches professing the Protestant faith.—GC 383 (1911).

Notwithstanding the spiritual darkness and alienation from God that exist in the churches which constitute Babylon, the great body of Christ's true followers are still to be found in their communion.—GC 390 (1911).

Babylon's Fall Not Yet Complete

"She made all nations drink of the wine of the wrath of her fornication" (Rev. 14:6-8). How is this done? By forcing men to accept a spurious sabbath.—8T 94 (1904).

Not yet, however, can it be said that . . . "she made *all nations* drink of the wine of the wrath of her fornication." She has not yet made all nations do this. . . .

Not until this condition shall be reached, and the union of the church with the world shall be fully accomplished throughout Christendom, will the fall of Babylon be complete. The change is a progressive one, and the perfect fulfillment of Revelation 14:8 is yet future.—GC 389, 390 (1911).

When do her sins reach unto heaven [Rev. 18:2-5]? When the law of God is finally made void by legislation.—ST June 12, 1893.

God's Last Warning Message

God has given the messages of Revelation 14 their place in the line of prophecy and their work is not to cease till the close of this earth's history.—EGW'88 804 (1890).

Revelation 18 points to the time when, as the result of rejecting the threefold warning of Revelation 14:6-12, the church will have fully reached the condition foretold by the second angel, and the people of God still in Babylon will be called upon to separate from her communion. This message is the last that will ever be given to the world.—GC 390 (1911).

[Rev. 18:1, 2, 4, quoted.] This scripture points forward to a time when the announcement of the fall of Babylon, as made by the second angel of Revelation 14 (verse 8), is to be repeated, with the additional mention of the corruptions which have been entering the various organizations that constitute Babylon, since that message was first given, in the summer of 1844. . . . These announcements, uniting with the third angel's message, constitute the final warning to be given to the inhabitants of the earth. . . .

The sins of Babylon will be laid open. The fearful results of enforcing the observances of the church by civil authority, the inroads of spiritualism, the stealthy but rapid progress of the papal power—all will be unmasked. By these solemn warnings the people will be stirred. Thousands upon thousands will listen who have never heard words like these.—GC 603, 604, 606 (1911).

The Heart of God's Last Message

Several have written to me, inquiring if the message of justification by faith is the third angel's message, and I have answered, "It is the third angel's message in verity."—1SM 372 (1890).

The Lord in His great mercy sent a most precious message to His people through Elders [E. J.] Waggoner and [A. T.] Jones. This message was to bring more prominently before the world the uplifted Saviour, the sacrifice for the sins of the whole world. It presented justification through faith in the Surety; it invited the people to receive the righteousness of Christ, which is made manifest in obedience to all the commandments of God.

Many had lost sight of Jesus. They needed to have their eyes directed to His divine person, His merits, and His changeless love for the human family. All power is given into His hands, that He may dispense rich gifts unto men, imparting the priceless gift of His own righteousness to the helpless human agent. This is the message that God commanded to be given to the world. It is the third angel's message, which is to be proclaimed with a loud voice, and attended with the outpouring of His Spirit in a large measure.—TM 91, 92 (1895).

The message of Christ's righteousness is to sound from one end of the earth to the other to prepare the way of the Lord. This is the glory of God, which closes the work of the third angel.—6T 19 (1900).

The last message of mercy to be given to the world is a revelation of His character of love. The children of God are to manifest His glory. In their own life and character they are to reveal what the grace of God has done for them.—COL 415, 416 (1900).

The Message Will Go With Great Power

As the third message swells to a loud cry and as great power and glory attend the closing work, the faithful people of God will partake of that glory. It is the latter rain which revives and strengthens them to pass through the time of trouble.—7BC 984 (1862).

As the end approaches, the testimonies of God's servants will become more decided and more powerful.—3SM 407 (1892).

This message [Rev. 14:9-12] embraces the two preceding messages. It is represented as being given with a loud voice; that is, with the power of the Holy Spirit.—7BC 980 (1900).

As the third angel's message swells into a loud cry, great power and glory will attend its proclamation. The faces of God's people will shine with the light of heaven.—7T 17 (1902).

Amidst the deepening shadows of earth's last great crisis, God's light will shine brightest, and the song of hope and trust will be heard in clearest and loftiest strains.—Ed 166 (1903).

As foretold in the eighteenth of Revelation, the third angel's message is to be proclaimed with great power by those who give the final warning against the beast and his image.—8T 118 (1904).

Like the 1844 Movement

The power which stirred the people so mightily in the 1844 movement will again be revealed. The third angel's message will go forth, not in whispered tones, but with a loud voice.—5T 252 (1885).

I saw that this message will close with power and strength far exceeding the midnight cry.—EW 278 (1858).

Like the Day of Pentecost

It is with an earnest longing that I look forward to the time when the events of the Day of Pentecost shall be repeated with even greater power than on that occasion. John says, "I saw another angel come down from heaven, having great power; and the earth was lightened with his glory" [Rev. 18:1]. Then, as at the Pentecostal season, the people will hear the truth spoken to them, every man in his own tongue.—6BC 1055 (1886).

In visions of the night, representations passed before me of a great reformatory movement among God's people. Many were praising God. The sick were healed, and other miracles were wrought. A spirit of intercession was seen, even as was manifested before the great Day of Pentecost.—9T 126 (1909).

The great work of the gospel is not to close with less manifestation of the power of God than marked its opening. The prophecies which were fulfilled in the outpouring of the former rain at the opening of the gospel, are again to be fulfilled in the latter rain at its close. . . .

Servants of God, with their faces lighted up and shining with holy consecration, will hasten from place to place to proclaim the message from heaven. By thousands of voices, all over the earth, the warning will be given. Miracles will be wrought, the sick will be healed, and signs and wonders will follow the believers. —GC 611, 612 (1911).

God Will Employ
Agencies That Will Surprise Us

Let me tell you that the Lord will work in this last work in a manner very much out of the common order of things, and in a way that will be contrary to any human planning. There will be those among us who will always want to control the work of God, to dictate even what movements shall be made when the work goes forward under the direction of the angel who joins the third angel in the message to be given to the world. God will use ways and means by which it will be seen that He is taking the reins in His own hands. The workers will be surprised by the simple means that He will use to bring about and perfect His work of righteousness.—TM 300 (1885).

Do not imagine that it will be possible to lay out plans for the future. Let God be acknowledged as standing at the helm at all times and under every circumstance. He will work by means that will be suitable, and will maintain, increase, and build up His own people.—CW 71 (1895).

The Comforter is to reveal Himself, not in any specified, precise way that man may mark out, but in the order of God—in unexpected times and ways that will honor His own name.—EGW'88 1478 (1896).

He will raise up from among the common people men and women to do His work, even as of old He called fishermen to be His disciples. There will soon be an awakening that will surprise many. Those who do not realize the necessity of what is to be done will be passed by, and the heavenly messengers will work with those who are called the common people, fitting them to carry the truth to many places.—15MR 312 (1905).

Laborers Qualified by the Holy Spirit

In the last solemn work few great men will be engaged. . . . God will work a work in our day that but few anticipate. He will raise up and exalt among us those who are taught rather by the unction of His Spirit than by the outward training of scientific institutions. These facilities are not to be despised or condemned; they are ordained of God, but they can furnish only the exterior qualifications. God will manifest that He is not dependent on learned, self-important mortals.—5T 80, 82 (1882).

To souls that are earnestly seeking for light and that accept with gladness every ray of divine illumination from His holy Word, to such alone light will be given. It is through these souls that God will reveal that light and power which will lighten the whole earth with His glory.—5T 729 (1889).

It is discipline of spirit, cleanness of heart and thought that is needed. This is of more value than brilliant talent, tact, or knowledge. An ordinary mind, trained to obey a "Thus saith the Lord," is better qualified for God's work than are those who have capabilities but do not employ them rightly.—RH Nov. 27, 1900.

The laborers will be qualified rather by the unction of His Spirit than by the training of literary institutions. Men of faith and prayer will be constrained to go forth with holy zeal, declaring the words which God gives them.—GC 606 (1911).

God Uses Even the Illiterate

Those who receive Christ as a personal Saviour will stand the test and trial of these last days. Strengthened by unquestioning faith in Christ, even the illiterate disciple will be able to withstand the doubts and questions that infidelity can produce, and put to blush the sophistries of scorners.

The Lord Jesus will give the disciples a tongue and wisdom that their adversaries can neither gainsay nor resist. Those who could not, by reasoning, overcome satanic delusions will bear an affirmative testimony that will baffle supposedly learned men. Words will come from the lips of the unlearned with such convincing power and wisdom that conversions will be made to the truth. Thousands will be converted under their testimony.

Why should the illiterate man have this power, which the learned man has not? The illiterate one, through faith in Christ, has come into the atmosphere of pure, clear truth, while the learned man has turned away from the truth. The poor man is Christ's witness. He cannot appeal to histories or to so-called high science, but he gathers from the Word of God powerful evidence. The truth that he speaks under the inspiration of the Spirit is so pure and remarkable and carries with it a power so indisputable that his testimony cannot be gainsaid.—8MR 187, 188 (1905).

Children Proclaim the Message

Many, even among the uneducated, now proclaim the words of the Lord. Children are impelled by the Spirit to go forth and declare the message from heaven. The Spirit is poured out upon all who will yield to its promptings and, casting off all man's machinery, his binding rules and cautious methods, they will declare the truth with the might of the Spirit's power.—Ev 700 (1895).

When the heavenly intelligences see that men will no longer present the truth in simplicity as did Jesus, the very children will be moved upon by the Spirit of

God and will go forth proclaiming the truth for this time.—SW 66 (1895).

The Ministry of Angels

The angels of heaven are moving upon human minds to arouse investigation in the themes of the Bible. A far greater work will be done than has yet been done and none of the glory of it will flow to men, for angels that minister to those who shall be heirs of salvation are working night and day.—CW 140 (1875).

There are many men in our world who are like Cornelius. . . . As God worked for Cornelius, so He works for these true standard-bearers. . . . They will obtain a knowledge of God as Cornelius did through the visitation of angels from heaven.—Letter 197, 1904.

When divine power is combined with human effort, the work will spread like fire in the stubble. God will employ agencies whose origin man will be unable to discern. Angels will do a work which men might have had the blessing of accomplishing had they not neglected to answer the claims of God.—1SM 118 (1885).

World-wide Extent of the Proclamation

The angel who unites in the proclamation of the third angel's message is to lighten the whole earth with his glory. A work of world-wide extent and unwonted power is here foretold. . . . Servants of God, with their faces lighted up and shining with holy consecration, will hasten from place to place to proclaim the message from heaven. By thousands of voices, all over the earth, the warning will be given. —GC 611, 612 (1911).

The message of the angel following the third is now to be given to all parts of the world. It is to be the harvest message, and the whole earth will be lighted with the glory of God.—Letter 86, 1900.

When the storm of persecution really breaks upon us, . . . then will the message of the third angel swell to a loud cry, and the whole earth will be lightened with the glory of the Lord.—6T 401 (1900).

In every city in America the truth is to be proclaimed. In every country of the world the warning message is to be given.—GCB March 30, 1903.

During the loud cry the church, aided by the providential interpositions of her exalted Lord, will diffuse the knowledge of salvation so abundantly that light will be communicated to every city and town. —Ev 694 (1904).

A crisis is right upon us. We must now by the Holy Spirit's power proclaim the great truths for these last days. It will not be long before everyone will have heard the warning and made his decision. Then shall the end come.—6T 24 (1900).

Kings, Legislators,
Councils, Hear the Message

It does not seem possible to us now that any should have to stand alone, but if God has ever spoken by me, the time will come when we shall be brought before councils and before thousands for His name's sake, and each one will have to give the reason of his faith. Then will come the severest criticism upon every position that has been taken for the truth. We need, then, to study the Word of God, that we may know why we believe the doctrines we advocate.—RH Dec. 18, 1888.

Many will have to stand in the legislative courts; some will have to stand before kings and before the learned of the earth to answer for their faith. Those who have only a superficial understanding of truth will not be able clearly to expound the Scriptures and give definite reasons for their faith. They will become confused and will not be workmen that need not to be ashamed. Let no one imagine that he has no need to study because he is not to preach in the sacred desk. You know not what God may require of you.—FE 217 (1893).

Many Adventists Brace
Themselves Against the Light

There is to be in the [Seventh-day Adventist] churches a wonderful manifestation of the power of God, but it will not move upon those who have not humbled themselves before the Lord, and opened the door of the heart by confession and repentance. In the

manifestation of that power which lightens the earth
with the glory of God, they will see only something
which in their blindness they think dangerous, something which will arouse their fears, and they will
brace themselves to resist it. Because the Lord does
not work according to their ideas and expectations
they will oppose the work. "Why," they say, "should we
not know the Spirit of God, when we have been in the
work so many years?"—RH Extra, Dec. 23, 1890.

The third angel's message will not be compre-
hended, the light which will lighten the earth with its
glory will be called a false light, by those who refuse
to walk in its advancing glory.—RH May 27, 1890.

Most Non-Adventists Will Reject the Warning

Many who hear the message—by far the greatest
number—will not credit the solemn warning. Many
will be found disloyal to the commandments of God,
which are a test of character. The Lord's servants will
be called enthusiasts. Ministers will warn the people
not to listen to them. Noah received the same treat-
ment while the Spirit of God was urging him to give
the message, whether men would hear or whether
they would forbear.—TM 233 (1895).

Some will listen to these warnings, but by the vast
majority they will be disregarded.—HP 343 (1897).

The popular ministry, like the Pharisees of old,
filled with anger as their authority is questioned, will

denounce the message as of Satan, and stir up the sin-loving multitudes to revile and persecute those who proclaim it.—GC 607 (1911).

Multitudes Will Answer the Call

Souls that were scattered all through the religious bodies answered to the call, and the precious were hurried out of the doomed churches, as Lot was hurried out of Sodom before her destruction.—EW 279 (1858).

There will be an army of steadfast believers who will stand as firm as a rock through the last test. —3SM 390 (1888).

There are many souls to come out of the ranks of the world, out of the churches—even the Catholic Church—whose zeal will far exceed that of those who have stood in rank and file to proclaim the truth heretofore.—3SM 386, 387 (1889).

Multitudes will receive the faith and join the armies of the Lord.—Ev 700 (1895).

Many who have strayed from the fold will come back to follow the great Shepherd.—6T 401 (1900).

In heathen Africa, in the Catholic lands of Europe and of South America, in China, in India, in the islands of the sea, and in all the dark corners of the earth, God has in reserve a firmament of chosen ones that will yet shine forth amidst the darkness, revealing clearly to an apostate world the transforming power of obedience to His law. Even now they are appearing in every nation, among every tongue and people; and in the hour of deepest apostasy, when Satan's supreme effort is made to cause "all, both small and great, rich and poor, free and bond," to receive, under penalty of death, the sign of allegiance to a false rest day, these faithful ones, "blameless and harmless, the sons of God, without rebuke," will "shine as lights in the world."—PK 188, 189 (c. 1914).

Thousands Converted in a Day

Thousands in the eleventh hour will see and acknowledge the truth. . . . These conversions to truth will be made with a rapidity that will surprise the church, and God's name alone will be glorified.—2SM 16 (1890).

There will be thousands converted to the truth in a day who at the eleventh hour see and acknowledge the truth and the movements of the Spirit of God.—EGW'88 755 (1890).

The time is coming when there will be as many converted in a day as there were on the Day of Pentecost, after the disciples had received the Holy Spirit.—Ev 692 (1905).

The Honest-in-Heart Will Not Hesitate Long

A good many do not see it now, to take their position, but these things are influencing their lives, and when the message goes with a loud voice they will be ready for it. They will not hesitate long; they will come out and take their position.—Ev 300, 301 (1890).

Soon the last test is to come to all inhabitants of the earth. At that time prompt decisions will be made. Those who have been convicted under the presentation of the Word will range themselves under the bloodstained banner of Prince Emmanuel.—9T 149 (1909).

Every truly honest soul will come to the light of truth.—GC 522 (1911).

The message will be carried not so much by argument as by the deep conviction of the Spirit of God. The arguments have been presented. The seed has been sown, and now it will spring up and bear fruit. The publications distributed by missionary workers have exerted their influence, yet many whose minds were impressed have been prevented from fully comprehending the truth or from yielding obedience. Now the rays of light penetrate everywhere, the truth is seen in its clearness, and the honest children of God sever the bands which have held them. Family connections, church relations, are powerless to stay them now. Truth is more precious than all besides. Notwithstanding the agencies combined against the truth, a large number take their stand upon the Lord's side.—GC 612 (1911).

Influence of the Printed Page

More than one thousand will soon be converted in one day, most of whom will trace their first convictions to the reading of our publications.—Ev 693 (1885).

The results of the circulation of this book [*The Great Controversy*] are not to be judged by what now appears. By reading it some souls will be aroused and will have courage to unite themselves at once with those who keep the commandments of God. But a much larger number who read it will not take their position until they see the very events taking place that are foretold in it. The fulfillment of some of the predictions will inspire faith that others also will come to pass, and when the earth is lightened with the glory of the Lord in the closing work, many souls will take their position on the commandments of God as the result of this agency.—CM 128, 129 (1890).

In a large degree through our publishing houses is to be accomplished the work of that other angel who comes down from heaven with great power and who lightens the earth with his glory [Rev. 18:1]. —7T 140 (1902).

15.

The Seal of God and the Mark of the Beast

Only Two Classes

There can be only two classes. Each party is distinctly stamped, either with the seal of the living God, or with the mark of the beast or his image.—RH Jan. 30, 1900.

In the great conflict between faith and unbelief the whole Christian world will be involved. All will take sides. Some apparently may not engage in the conflict on either side. They may not appear to take sides against the truth, but they will not come out boldly for Christ through fear of losing property or suffering reproach. All such are numbered with the enemies of Christ.—RH Feb. 7, 1893.

As we near the close of time the demarcation between the children of light and the children of darkness will be more and more decided. They will be more and more at variance. This difference is expressed in the words of Christ, "born again"—created anew in Christ, dead to the world, and alive unto God. These are the walls of separation that divide the heavenly from the earthly and describe the difference between those who belong to the world and those who are chosen out of it, who are elect, precious in the sight of God.—*Special Testimony to the Battle Creek Church* (Ph 155) 3 (1882).

Family Members Are Separated

Those who have been members of the same family are separated. A mark is placed upon the righteous. "They shall be Mine, saith the Lord of hosts, in that day when I make up My jewels; and I will spare them, as a man spareth his own son that serveth him" [Mal. 3:17]. Those who have been obedient to God's commandments will unite with the company of the saints in light. They shall enter in through the gates into the city, and have right to the tree of life.

"The one shall be taken." His name shall stand in the book of life, while those with whom he associated shall have the mark of eternal separation from God. —TM 234, 235 (1895).

Judged by the Light We Have Received

Many who have not had the privileges that we have had will go into heaven before those who have had great light and who have not walked in it. Many have lived up to the best light they have had and will be judged accordingly.—Letter 36, 1895.

All must wait for the appointed time, until the warning shall have gone to all parts of the world, until sufficient light and evidence have been given to every soul. Some will have less light than others, but each one will be judged according to the light received. —Ms 77, 1899.

We have been given great light in regard to God's law. This law is the standard of character. To it man is now required to conform, and by it he will be judged in the last great day. In that day men will be dealt with according to the light they have received.—GH Jan. 1901.

Those who have had great light and have disregarded it stand in a worse position than those who have not been given so many advantages. They exalt themselves but not the Lord. The punishment inflicted on human beings will in every case be proportionate to the dishonor they have brought on God. —8MR 168 (1901).

Everyone is to have sufficient light to make his decision intelligently.—GC 605 (1911).

No Excuse for Willful Blindness

None will be condemned for not heeding light and knowledge that they never had, and they could not obtain. But many refuse to obey the truth that is presented to them by Christ's ambassadors, because they wish to conform to the world's standard, and the truth that has reached their understanding, the light that has shone in the soul, will condemn them in the judgment.—5BC 1145 (1884).

Those who have an opportunity to hear the truth and yet take no pains to hear or understand it, thinking that if they do not hear they will not be accountable, will be judged guilty before God the same as if they had heard and rejected. There will be no excuse for those who choose to go in error when they might understand what is truth. In His sufferings and death Jesus has made atonement for all sins of ignorance, but there is no provision made for willful blindness.

We shall not be held accountable for the light that has not reached our perception, but for that which we have resisted and refused. A man could not apprehend the truth which had never been presented to him, and therefore could not be condemned for light he had never had.—5BC 1145 (1893).

The Importance of Practical Benevolence

The decisions of the last day turn upon our practical benevolence. Christ acknowledges every act of beneficence as done to Himself.—TM 400 (1896).

When the nations are gathered before Him, there will be but two classes, and their eternal destiny will be determined by what they have done or have neglected to do for Him in the person of the poor and suffering. . . .

Among the heathen are those who worship God ignorantly, those to whom the light is never brought by human instrumentality, yet they will not perish.

Though ignorant of the written law of God, they have heard His voice speaking to them in nature, and have done the things that the law required. Their works are evidence that the Holy Spirit has touched their hearts, and they are recognized as the children of God.

How surprised and gladdened will be the lowly among the nations, and among the heathen, to hear from the lips of the Saviour, "Inasmuch as ye have done it unto one of the least of these My brethren, ye have done it unto Me"! How glad will be the heart of Infinite Love as His followers look up with surprise and joy at His words of approval!—DA 637, 638 (1898).

Motive Gives Character to Actions

In the day of judgment some will plead this good deed and that as a reason why they should receive consideration. They will say, "I set up young men in business. I gave money to found hospitals. I relieved the necessities of widows, and took the poor into my home." Yes, but your motives were so defiled by selfishness that the deed was not acceptable in the sight of the Lord. In all that you did, self was brought prominently to view.—Ms 53, 1906.

It is the motive that gives character to our acts, stamping them with ignominy or with high moral worth.—DA 615 (1898).

What the Seal of God Is

Just as soon as the people of God are sealed in their foreheads—it is not any seal or mark that can be seen, but a settling into the truth, both intellectually and spiritually, so they cannot be moved—just as soon as God's people are sealed and prepared for the shaking, it will come. Indeed, it has begun already.—4BC 1161 (1902).

The seal of the living God is placed upon those who conscientiously keep the Sabbath of the Lord.[1]—7BC 980 (1897).

Those who would have the seal of God in their foreheads must keep the Sabbath of the fourth commandment.—7BC 970 (1899).

True observance of the Sabbath is the sign of loyalty to God.—7BC 981 (1899).

The fourth commandment alone of all the ten contains the seal of the great Lawgiver, the Creator of the heavens and the earth.—6T 350 (1900).

The observance of the Lord's memorial, the Sabbath instituted in Eden, the seventh-day Sabbath, is the test of our loyalty to God.—Letter 94, 1900.

A mark is placed upon every one of God's people, just as verily as a mark was placed over the doors of the Hebrew dwellings to preserve the people from the

1. This statement and others like it should be understood in the light of passages quoted earlier in the chapter, indicating that God holds people responsible only for the knowledge they have or which they could obtain.

general ruin. God declares, "I gave them My sabbaths, to be a sign between Me and them, that they might know that I am the Lord that sanctify them" [Eze. 20:12].—7BC 969 (1900).

A Likeness to Christ in Character

The seal of the living God will be placed upon those only who bear a likeness to Christ in character.—7BC 970 (1895).

Those who receive the seal of the living God and are protected in the time of trouble must reflect the image of Jesus fully.—EW 71 (1851).

The seal of God will never be placed upon the forehead of an impure man or woman. It will never be placed upon the forehead of the ambitious, world-loving man or woman. It will never be placed upon the forehead of men or women of false tongues or deceitful hearts. All who receive the seal must be without spot before God—candidates for heaven.—5T 216 (1882).

Love is expressed in obedience, and perfect love casteth out all fear. Those who love God, have the seal of God in their foreheads, and work the works of God.—SD 51 (1894).

Those that overcome the world, the flesh, and the devil, will be the favored ones who shall receive the seal of the living God.—TM 445 (c. 1886).

Are we striving with all our God-given powers to reach the measure of the stature of men and women in Christ? Are we seeking for His fullness, ever reaching higher and higher, trying to attain to the perfection of His character? When God's servants reach this point, they will be sealed in their foreheads. The recording angel will declare, "It is done." They will be complete in Him whose they are by creation and by redemption.—3SM 427 (1899).

In the Sealing Time Now

I saw that the present test on the Sabbath could not come until the mediation of Jesus in the holy place was finished and He had passed within the second veil; therefore Christians who fell asleep before the door was opened into the most holy, when the midnight cry was finished, at the seventh month, 1844, and who had not kept the true Sabbath, now rest in hope, for they had not the light and the test on the Sabbath which we now have since that door was opened. I saw that Satan was tempting some of God's people on this point. Because so many good Christians have fallen asleep in the triumphs of faith and have not kept the true Sabbath, they were doubting about its being a test for us now. . . .

Satan is now using every device in this sealing time to keep the minds of God's people from the present truth and to cause them to waver.—EW 42, 43 (1851).

I saw that she [Mrs. Hastings] was sealed and would come up at the voice of God and stand upon the earth, and would be with the 144,000. I saw we need not mourn for her; she would rest in the time of trouble.—2SM 263 (1850).

There are living upon our earth men who have passed the age of fourscore and ten. The natural results of old age are seen in their feebleness. But they believe God, and God loves them. The seal of God is upon them, and they will be among the number of whom the Lord has said, "Blessed are the dead which die in the Lord."—7BC 982 (1899).

Oh, That God's Seal May Be Placed Upon Us!

In a little while every one who is a child of God will have His seal placed upon him. Oh, that it may be placed upon our foreheads! Who can endure the thought of being passed by when the angel goes forth to seal the servants of God in their foreheads?—7BC 969, 970 (1889).

If the believers in the truth are not sustained by their faith in these comparatively peaceful days, what will uphold them when the grand test comes and the decree goes forth against all those who will not worship the image of the beast and receive his mark in their foreheads or in their hands? This solemn period is not far off. Instead of becoming weak and irresolute, the people of God should be gathering strength and courage for the time of trouble.—4T 251 (1876).

What the Mark of the Beast Is

John was called to behold a people distinct from those who worship the beast or his image by keeping the first day of the week. The observance of this day is the mark of the beast.—TM 133 (1898).

The mark of the beast is the papal sabbath.—Ev 234 (1899).

When the test comes, it will be clearly shown what the mark of the beast is. It is the keeping of Sunday. —7BC 980 (1900).

The sign, or seal, of God is revealed in the observance of the seventh-day Sabbath, the Lord's memorial of creation. . . . The mark of the beast is the opposite of this—the observance of the first day of the week. —8T 117 (1904).

"He causeth all, both small and great, . . . to receive a mark in their right hand, or in their foreheads" (Rev. 13:16). Not only are men not to work with their hands on Sunday, but with their minds are they to acknowledge Sunday as the Sabbath.—*Special Testimony to Battle Creek Church* (Ph 86) 6, 7 (1897).

When the Mark of the Beast Is Received

No one has yet received the mark of the beast.—Ev 234 (1899).

Sundaykeeping is not yet the mark of the beast, and will not be until the decree goes forth causing men to worship this idol sabbath. The time will come when this day will be the test, but that time has not come yet.—7BC 977 (1899).

God has given men the Sabbath as a sign between Him and them as a test of their loyalty. Those who, after the light regarding God's law comes to them, continue to disobey and exalt human laws above the law of God in the great crisis before us, will receive the mark of the beast.—Ev 235 (1900).

The Sabbath will be the great test of loyalty, for it is the point of truth especially controverted. When the final test shall be brought to bear upon men, then the line of distinction will be drawn between those who serve God and those who serve Him not.

While the observance of the false sabbath in compliance with the law of the state, contrary to the fourth commandment, will be an avowal of allegiance to a power that is in opposition to God, the keeping of the true Sabbath, in obedience to God's law, is an evidence of loyalty to the Creator. While one class, by accepting the sign of submission to earthly powers, receive the mark of the beast, the other, choosing the token of allegiance to divine authority, receive the seal of God.—GC 605 (1911).

Enforcement of Sunday Observance Is the Test

None are condemned until they have had the light and have seen the obligation of the fourth commandment. But when the decree shall go forth enforcing the

counterfeit sabbath, and the loud cry of the third
angel shall warn men against the worship of the beast
and his image, the line will be clearly drawn between
the false and the true. Then those who still continue
in transgression will receive the mark of the beast.
—Ev 234, 235 (1899).

When Sunday observance shall be enforced by law,
and the world shall be enlightened concerning the
obligation of the true Sabbath, then whoever shall
transgress the command of God to obey a precept
which has no higher authority than that of Rome, will
thereby honor popery above God. He is paying homage to Rome, and to the power which enforces the
institution ordained by Rome. He is worshiping the
beast and his image.

As men then reject the institution which God has
declared to be the sign of His authority, and honor in
its stead that which Rome has chosen as the token of
her supremacy, they will thereby accept the sign of
allegiance to Rome—"the mark of the beast." And it is
not until the issue is thus plainly set before the people,
and they are brought to choose between the commandments of God and the commandments of men,
that those who continue in transgression will receive
"the mark of the beast."—GC 449 (1911).

16.

The Close of Probation

No One Knows When Probation Will Close

God has not revealed to us the time when this message will close or when probation will have an end. Those things that are revealed we shall accept for ourselves and for our children, but let us not seek to know that which has been kept secret in the councils of the Almighty. . . .

Letters have come to me asking me if I have any special light as to the time when probation will close, and I answer that I have only this message to bear, that it is now time to work while the day lasts, for the night cometh in which no man can work.—1SM 191 (1894).

Sunday-Law Enforcement Precedes the Close of Probation

The Lord has shown me clearly that the image of the beast will be formed before probation closes, for it is to be the great test[1] for the people of God, by which

---

1. See the previous chapter, where the great test for the people of God is shown to be Sunday-law enforcement.

their eternal destiny will be decided.—2SM 81 (1890).

What is the "image to the beast"? and how is it to be formed? The image is made by the two-horned beast, and is an image *to* the beast. It is also called an image *of* the beast.[2] Then to learn what the image is like and how it is to be formed, we must study the characteristics of the beast itself—the papacy.

When the early church became corrupted by departing from the simplicity of the gospel and accepting heathen rites and customs, she lost the Spirit and power of God; and in order to control the consciences of the people, she sought the support of the secular power. The result was the papacy, a church that controlled the power of the state, and employed it to further her own ends, especially for the punishment of "heresy." In order for the United States to form an image of the beast, the religious power must so control the civil government that the authority of the state will also be employed by the church to accomplish her own ends. . . .

The "image to the beast" represents that form of apostate Protestantism which will be developed when the Protestant churches shall seek the aid of the civil power for the enforcement of their dogmas.—GC 443, 445 (1911).

Probation Closes
When the Sealing Is Finished

Just before we entered it [the time of trouble], we all received the seal of the living God. Then I saw the four

_____
2. The two-horned beast of Revelation 13:11-17 makes an image to the beast portrayed in Revelation 13:1-10.

angels cease to hold the four winds. And I saw famine, pestilence and sword, nation rose against nation, and the whole world was in confusion.—7BC 968 (1846).

I saw angels hurrying to and fro in heaven. An angel with a writer's inkhorn by his side returned from the earth and reported to Jesus that his work was done, and the saints were numbered and sealed. Then I saw Jesus, who had been ministering before the ark containing the ten commandments, throw down the censer. He raised His hands, and with a loud voice said, *"It is done."*—EW 279 (1858).

Only a moment of time, as it were, yet remains. But while already nation is rising against nation and kingdom against kingdom, there is not now a general engagement. As yet the four winds are held until the servants of God shall be sealed in their foreheads. Then the powers of earth will marshal their forces for the last great battle.—6T 14 (1900).

An angel returning from the earth announces that his work is done; the final test has been brought upon the world, and all who have proved themselves loyal to the divine precepts have received "the seal of the living God." Then Jesus ceases His intercession in the sanctuary above. He lifts His hands, and with a loud voice says, "It is done."—GC 613 (1911).

Probation Will End Suddenly, Unexpectedly

When Jesus ceases to plead for man, the cases of all are forever decided. . . . Probation closes; Christ's intercessions cease in heaven. This time finally comes suddenly upon all, and those who have neglected to purify their souls by obeying the truth are found sleeping.—2T 191 (1868).

When probation ends, it will come suddenly, unex-pectedly—at a time when we are least expecting it. But we can have a clean record in heaven today, and know that God accepts us.—7BC 989 (1906).

When the work of the investigative judgment closes, the destiny of all will have been decided for life or death. Probation is ended a short time before the appearing of the Lord in the clouds of heaven. . . .

Before the Flood, after Noah entered the ark, God shut him in, and shut the ungodly out; but for seven days the people, knowing not that their doom was fixed, continued their careless, pleasure-loving life, and mocked the warnings of impending judgment. "So," says the Saviour, "shall also the coming of the Son of man be" (Matt. 24:39). Silently, unnoticed as the midnight thief, will come the decisive hour which marks the fixing of every man's destiny, the final withdrawal of mercy's offer to guilty men. . . .

While the man of business is absorbed in the pursuit of gain, while the pleasure lover is seeking indulgence, while the daughter of fashion is arrang-ing her adornments—it may be in that hour the Judge of all the earth will pronounce the sentence: "Thou art weighed in the balances, and art found wanting" (Dan. 5:27).—GC 490, 491 (1911).

Human Activity After Probation's Close

The righteous and the wicked will still be living upon the earth in their mortal state—men will be planting and building, eating and drinking, all unconscious that the final, irrevocable decision has been pronounced in the sanctuary above.—GC 491 (1911).

When the irrevocable decision of the sanctuary has been pronounced, and the destiny of the world has been forever fixed, the inhabitants of the earth will know it not. The forms of religion will be continued by a people from whom the Spirit of God has been finally withdrawn, and the satanic zeal with which the prince of evil will inspire them for the accomplishment of his malignant designs, will bear the semblance of zeal for God.—GC 615 (1911).

The wheat and tares "grow together until the harvest." In the discharge of life's duties the righteous will to the last be brought in contact with the ungodly. The children of light are scattered among the children of darkness, that the contrast may be seen by all. —5T 100 (1882).

Christ declared that when He comes some of His waiting people will be engaged in business transactions. Some will be sowing in the field, others reaping and gathering in the harvest, and others grinding at the mill.—Ms 26, 1901.

Unbelief and Forbidden Pleasures Continue

Skepticism and that which is called science has to a large degree undermined the faith of the Christian world in their Bibles. Error and fables are gladly accepted, that they may pursue the path of self-indulgence and not be alarmed, for they are striving not to retain God in their knowledge. They say, "Tomorrow will be as this day and much more abundant." But in the midst of their unbelief and godless pleasure the shout of the archangel and the trump of God is heard. . . .

When everything in our world is busy activity, immersed in selfish ambition for gain, Jesus comes as a thief.—Ms 15b, 1886.

When the professed people of God are uniting with the world, living as they live, and joining with them in forbidden pleasure; when the luxury of the world becomes the luxury of the church; when the marriage bells are chiming, and all are looking forward to many years of worldly prosperity—then, suddenly as the lightning flashes from the heavens, will come the end of their bright visions and delusive hopes.—GC 338, 339 (1911).

Men Will Be Wholly Engrossed in Business

When Lot warned the members of his family of the destruction of Sodom, they would not heed his words, but looked upon him as a fanatical enthusiast. The destruction that came found them unprepared. Thus it will be when Christ comes—farmers, merchants, lawyers, tradesmen, will be wholly engrossed in business, and upon them the day of the Lord will come as a snare.—RH March 10, 1904.

When ministers, farmers, merchants, lawyers, great men and professedly good men shall cry, "Peace and safety," sudden destruction cometh. Luke reports the words of Christ, that the day of God comes as a snare —the figure of an animal prowling in the woods for prey, and lo, suddenly he is entrapped in the concealed snare of the fowler.—10MR 266 (1876).

When men are at ease, full of amusement, absorbed in buying and selling, then the thief approaches with stealthy tread. So it will be at the coming of the Son of man.—Letter 21, 1897.

Religious Leaders Will Be Full of Optimism

When the reasoning of philosophy has banished the fear of God's judgments, when religious teachers are pointing forward to long ages of peace and prosperity, and the world are absorbed in their rounds of business and pleasure, planting and building, feasting and merrymaking, rejecting God's warnings and mocking His messengers—then it is that sudden destruction cometh upon them, and they shall not escape.—PP 104 (1890).

Come when it may, the day of God will come unawares to the ungodly. When life is going on in its unvarying round; when men are absorbed in pleasure, in business, in traffic, in money-making; when religious leaders are magnifying the world's progress and enlightenment, and the people are lulled in a false security—then, as the midnight thief steals within the unguarded dwelling, so shall sudden destruction come upon the careless and ungodly, "and they shall not escape."—GC 38 (1911).

Satan Infers That Probation Has Closed

In the time of trouble Satan stirs up the wicked, and they encircle the people of God to destroy them. But he does not know that "pardon" has been written opposite their names in the books of heaven.—RH Nov. 19, 1908.

As Satan influenced Esau to march against Jacob, so he will stir up the wicked to destroy God's people in the time of trouble. . . . He sees that holy angels are guarding them, and he infers that their sins have been pardoned, but he does not know that their cases have been decided in the sanctuary above.—GC 618 (1911).

A Famine for the Word

Those who do not now appreciate, study, and dearly prize the Word of God spoken by His servants will have cause to mourn bitterly hereafter. I saw that the Lord in judgment will at the close of time walk through the earth; the fearful plagues will begin to fall. Then those who have despised God's Word, those who have lightly esteemed it, shall "wander from sea to sea, and from the north even to the east; they shall run to and fro to seek the Word of the Lord and shall not find it" (Amos 8:12). A famine is in the land for hearing the Word.—Ms 1, 1857.

No More Prayers for the Wicked

The ministers of God will have done their last work, offered their last prayers, shed their last bitter tear for a rebellious church and an ungodly people. Their last solemn warning has been given. Oh, then how quickly would houses and lands, dollars that have been miserly hoarded and cherished and tightly grasped, be given for some consolation by those who have professed the truth and have not lived it out, for the way of salvation to be explained, or to hear a hopeful word or a prayer or an exhortation from their ministers. But no, they must hunger and thirst on in vain; their thirst will never be quenched, no consolation can they get. Their cases are decided and eternally fixed. It is a fearful, awful time.—Ms 1, 1857.

In the time when God's judgments are falling without mercy, oh, how enviable to the wicked will be the position of those who abide "in the secret place of the Most High"—the pavilion in which the Lord hides all who have loved Him and have obeyed His commandments! The lot of the righteous is indeed an enviable one at such a time to those who are suffering because of their sins. But the door of mercy is closed to the wicked. No more prayers are offered in their behalf after probation ends.—3BC 1150 (1901).

Transfer of Character Not Possible

The Lord is coming in power and great glory. It will then be His work to make a complete separation between the righteous and the wicked. But the oil cannot then be transferred to the vessels of those who have it not. Then shall be fulfilled the words of Christ, "Two women shall be grinding together; the one shall be taken, and the other left. Two men shall be in the field; the one shall be taken, and the other left." The righteous and the wicked are to be associated together in the work of life. But the Lord reads the character. He discerns who are obedient children, who respect and love His commandments.—TM 234 (1895).

It is a solemn thing to die, but a far more solemn thing to live. Every thought and word and deed of our lives will meet us again. What we make of ourselves in probationary time, that we must remain to all eternity. Death brings dissolution to the body, but makes no change in the character. The coming of Christ does not change our characters; it only fixes them forever beyond all change.—5T 466 (1885).

Another Probation Would
Not Convince the Wicked

We are to make the best of our present opportunities. There will be no other probation given to us in which to prepare for heaven. This is our only and last opportunity to form characters which will fit us for the future home which the Lord has prepared for all who are obedient to His commandments.—Letter 20, 1899.

There will be no probation after the coming of the Lord. Those who say that there will be are deceived and misled. Before Christ comes just such a state of things will exist as existed before the Flood. And after the Saviour appears in the clouds of heaven no one will be given another chance to gain salvation. All will have made their decisions.—Letter 45, 1891.

All will be tested and tried according to the light they have had. Those who turn from the truth to fables can look for no second probation. There will be no temporal millennium. If, after the Holy Spirit has brought conviction to their hearts, they resist the truth and use their influence to block the way so that others will not receive it, they will never be convinced. They did not seek for transformation of character in the probation given them, and Christ will not give them opportunity to pass over the ground again. The decision is a final one.—Letter 25, 1900.

17.

The Seven Last Plagues and the Wicked

(The Great Time of Trouble, Part 1)

The Vials of God's Wrath Will Be Poured Out

Solemn events before us are yet to transpire. Trumpet after trumpet is to be sounded; vial after vial poured out one after another upon the inhabitants of the earth.—3SM 426 (1890).

The world is soon to be left by the angel of mercy and the seven last plagues are to be poured out.... The bolts of God's wrath are soon to fall, and when He shall begin to punish the transgressors there will be no period of respite until the end.—TM 182 (1894).

The Nations in Conflict

Four mighty angels hold back the powers of this earth till the servants of God are sealed in their foreheads. The nations of the world are eager for conflict, but they are held in check by the angels. When this restraining power is removed there will come a time of trouble and anguish. Deadly instruments of warfare will be invented. Vessels with their living cargo will be entombed in the great deep. All who have not the spirit of truth will unite under the leadership of satanic agencies, but they are to be kept under control till the time shall come for the great battle of Armageddon.—7BC 967 (1900).

The Whole World Will Be Involved in Ruin

Angels are now restraining the winds of strife that they may not blow until the world shall be warned of its coming doom, but a storm is gathering, ready to burst upon the earth, and when God shall bid His angels loose the winds there will be such a scene of strife as no pen can picture.—Ed 179, 180 (1903).

The Saviour's prophecy concerning the visitation of judgments upon Jerusalem is to have another fulfillment, of which that terrible desolation was but a faint shadow. In the fate of the chosen city we may behold the doom of a world that has rejected God's mercy and trampled upon His law.—GC 36 (1911).

Satan will then plunge the inhabitants of the earth into one great, final trouble. As the angels of God cease to hold in check the fierce winds of human passion, all the elements of strife will be let loose. The whole world will be involved in ruin more terrible than that which came upon Jerusalem of old.—GC 614 (1911).

God Is Just, as Well as Merciful

It is the glory of God to be merciful, full of forbearance, kindness, goodness, and truth. But the justice shown in punishing the sinner is as verily the glory of the Lord as is the manifestation of His mercy.—RH March 10, 1904.

The Lord God of Israel is to execute judgment upon the gods of this world as upon the gods of Egypt. With fire and flood, plagues and earthquakes, He will spoil the whole land. Then His redeemed people will exalt His name and make it glorious in the earth. Shall not those who are living in the last remnant of this earth's history become intelligent in regard to God's lessons?—10MR 240, 241 (1899).

The One who has stood as our Intercessor; who hears all penitential prayers and confessions; who is represented with a rainbow, the symbol of grace and love, encircling His head, is soon to cease His work in the heavenly sanctuary. Grace and mercy will then descend from the throne, and justice will take their place. He for whom His people have looked will assume His right—the office of Supreme Judge.—RH Jan. 1, 1889.

In all the Bible, God is presented not only as a Being of mercy and benevolence, but as a God of strict and impartial justice.—ST March 24, 1881.

The Certainty of God's Judgments

God's love is represented in our day as being of such

a character as would forbid His destroying the sinner. Men reason from their own low standard of right and justice. "Thou thoughtest that I was altogether such an one as thyself" (Ps. 50:21). They measure God by themselves. They reason as to how they would act under the circumstances and decide God would do as they imagine they would do. . . .

In no kingdom or government is it left to the lawbreakers to say what punishment is to be executed against those who have broken the law. All we have, all the bounties of His grace which we possess, we owe to God. The aggravating character of sin against such a God cannot be estimated any more than the heavens can be measured with a span. God is a moral governor as well as a Father. He is the Lawgiver. He makes and executes His laws. Law that has no penalty is of no force.

The plea may be made that a loving Father would not see His children suffering the punishment of God by fire while He had the power to relieve them. But God would, for the good of His subjects and for their safety, punish the transgressor. God does not work on the plan of man. He can do infinite justice that man has no right to do before his fellow man. Noah would have displeased God to have drowned one of the scoffers and mockers that harassed him, but God drowned the vast world. Lot would have had no right to inflict punishment on his sons-in-law, but God would do it in strict justice.

Who will say God will not do what He says He will do?—12MR 207-209; 10MR 265 (1876).

Judgments Come When
God Removes His Protection

I was shown that the judgments of God would not come directly out from the Lord upon them, but in this way: They place themselves beyond His protection. He warns, corrects, reproves, and points out the only path of safety; then, if those who have been the objects of His special care will follow their own course, independent of the Spirit of God, after repeated warnings, if they choose their own way, then He does not commission His angels to prevent Satan's decided attacks upon them.

It is Satan's power that is at work at sea and on land, bringing calamity and distress and sweeping off multitudes to make sure of his prey.—14MR 3 (1883).

God will use His enemies as instruments to punish those who have followed their own pernicious ways whereby the truth of God has been misrepresented, misjudged, and dishonored.—PC 136 (1894).

Already the Spirit of God, insulted, refused, abused, is being withdrawn from the earth. Just as fast as God's Spirit is taken away, Satan's cruel work will be done upon land and sea.—Ms 134, 1898.

The wicked have passed the boundary of their probation; the Spirit of God, persistently resisted, has been at last withdrawn. Unsheltered by divine grace, they have no protection from the wicked one.—GC 614 (1911).

At Times Holy Angels
Exercise Destructive Power [1]

God's judgments were awakened against Jericho. It was a stronghold. But the Captain of the Lord's host Himself came from heaven to lead the armies of heaven in an attack upon the city. Angels of God laid hold of the massive walls and brought them to the ground.—3T 264 (1873).

Under God the angels are all-powerful. On one occasion, in obedience to the command of Christ, they slew of the Assyrian army in one night one hundred and eighty-five thousand men.—DA 700 (1898).

The same angel who had come from the royal courts to rescue Peter had been the messenger of wrath and judgment to Herod. The angel smote Peter to arouse him from slumber. It was with a different stroke that he smote the wicked king, laying low his pride and bringing upon him the punishment of the Almighty. Herod died in great agony of mind and body, under the retributive judgment of God.—AA 152 (1911).

A single angel destroyed all the first-born of the Egyptians and filled the land with mourning. When David offended against God by numbering the people, one angel caused that terrible destruction by which his

1. The sinner must himself bear full responsibility for the punishment that is meted out to him. Ellen White states, "God destroys no one. The sinner destroys himself by his own impenitence." 5T 120. See further *The Great Controversy*, pp. 25-37.

sin was punished. The same destructive power exercised by holy angels when God commands, will be exercised by evil angels when He permits. There are forces now ready, and only waiting the divine permission, to spread desolation everywhere.—GC 614 (1911).

The First Two Plagues

When Christ ceases His intercession in the sanctuary, the unmingled wrath threatened against those who worship the beast and his image and receive his mark (Rev. 14:9, 10), will be poured out. The plagues upon Egypt when God was about to deliver Israel, were similar in character to those more terrible and extensive judgments which are to fall upon the world just before the final deliverance of God's people. Says the revelator, in describing those terrific scourges: "There fell a noisome and grievous sore upon the men which had the mark of the beast, and upon them which worshiped his image." The sea "became as the blood of a dead man: and every living soul died in the sea" [Rev. 16:2, 3].—GC 627, 628 (1911).

The plagues were falling upon the inhabitants of the earth. Some were denouncing God and cursing Him. Others rushed to the people of God and begged to be taught how they might escape His judgments. But the saints had nothing for them. The last tear for sinners had been shed, the last agonizing prayer offered, the last burden borne, the last warning given.—EW 281 (1858).

The Third Plague

I saw that the four angels would hold the four winds until Jesus' work was done in the sanctuary, and then will come the seven last plagues. These plagues enraged the wicked against the righteous; they thought that we had brought the judgments of God upon them and that if they could rid the earth of us the plagues would then be stayed. A decree went forth to slay the saints, which caused them to cry day and night for deliverance.—EW 36, 37 (1851).

And "the rivers and fountains of waters . . . became blood." Terrible as these inflictions are, God's justice stands fully vindicated. The angel of God declares: "Thou art righteous, O Lord, . . . because Thou hast judged thus. For they have shed the blood of saints and prophets, and Thou hast given them blood to drink; for they are worthy" (Rev. 16:2-6). By condemning the people of God to death, they have as truly incurred the guilt of their blood as if it had been shed by their hands.—GC 628 (1911).

The Fourth Plague

In the plague that follows, power is given to the sun "to scorch men with fire. And men were scorched with great heat" (Rev. 16:8, 9). The prophets thus describe the condition of the earth at this fearful time: "The land mourneth; . . . because the harvest of the field is perished. . . . All the trees of the field are withered: because joy is withered away from the sons of men."

"The seed is rotten under their clods, the garners are laid desolate. . . . How do the beasts groan! the herds of cattle are perplexed, because they have no pasture. . . . The rivers of water are dried up, and the fire hath devoured the pastures of the wilderness." "The songs of the temple shall be howlings in that day, saith the Lord God: there shall be many dead bodies in every place; they shall cast them forth with silence" (Joel 1:10-12, 17-20; Amos 8:3).

These plagues are not universal, or the inhabitants of the earth would be wholly cut off. Yet they will be the most awful scourges that have ever been known to mortals.—GC 628, 629 (1911).

The Fifth Plague

With shouts of triumph, jeering, and imprecation, throngs of evil men are about to rush upon their prey, when, lo, a dense blackness, deeper than the darkness of the night, falls upon the earth. Then a rainbow, shining with the glory from the throne of God, spans the heavens, and seems to encircle each praying company. The angry multitudes are suddenly arrested. Their mocking cries die away. The objects of their murderous rage are forgotten. With fearful forebodings they gaze upon the symbol of God's covenant, and long to be shielded from its overpowering brightness. . . .

It is at midnight that God manifests His power for the deliverance of His people. The sun appears, shining in its strength. Signs and wonders follow in quick succession. The wicked look with terror and amazement on the scene, while the righteous behold with solemn joy the tokens of their deliverance.—GC 635, 636 (1911).

God's Law Appears in the Sky

There appears against the sky a hand holding two tables of stone folded together. Says the prophet, "The heavens shall declare His righteousness: for God is judge Himself" (Ps. 50:6). That holy law, God's right-eousness, that amid thunder and flame was pro-claimed from Sinai as the guide of life, is now revealed to men as the rule of judgment. The hand opens the tables, and there are seen the precepts of the Decalogue, traced as with a pen of fire. The words are so plain that all can read them. Memory is aroused, the darkness of superstition and heresy is swept from every mind, and God's ten words, brief, comprehensive, and authorita-tive, are presented to the view of all the inhabitants of the earth.—GC 639 (1911).

The Lost Condemn Their False Shepherds

Church members who have seen the light and been convicted, but who have trusted the salvation of their souls to the minister, will learn in the day of God that no other soul can pay the ransom for their transgres-sion. A terrible cry will be raised, "I am lost, eternally lost." Men will feel as though they could rend in pieces the ministers who have preached falsehoods and condemned the truth.—4BC 1157 (1900).

All unite in heaping their bitterest condemnation upon the ministers. Unfaithful pastors have prophesied smooth things; they have led their hearers to make void the law of God and to persecute those who would keep it holy. Now, in their despair, these teachers confess before the world their work of deception. The multitudes are filled with fury. "We are lost!" they cry, "and you are the cause of our ruin"; and they turn upon the false shepherds. The very ones that once admired them most, will pronounce the most dreadful curses upon them. The very hands that once crowned them with laurels, will be raised for their destruction. The swords which were to slay God's people, are now employed to destroy their enemies.—GC 655, 656 (1911).

Here we see that the church—the Lord's sanctuary—was the first to feel the stroke of the wrath of God. The ancient men [Eze. 9:6], those to whom God had given great light and who had stood as guardians of the spiritual interests of the people, had betrayed their trust.—5T 211 (1882).

God's Word is made of none effect by false shepherds. . . . Their work will soon react upon themselves. Then will be witnessed the scenes described in Revelation 18 when the judgments of God shall fall upon mystical Babylon.—Ms 60, 1900.

The Sixth Plague

The spirits of devils will go forth to the kings of the earth and to the whole world, to fasten them in deception, and urge them on to unite with Satan in his last struggle against the government of heaven.—GC 624 (1911).

The Spirit of God is gradually withdrawing from the world. Satan is also mustering his forces of evil, going forth "unto the kings of the earth and of the whole world," to gather them under his banner, to be trained for "the battle of that great day of God Almighty" [Rev. 16:14].—7BC 983 (1890).

After John's description in Revelation 16 of that miracle-working power which was to gather the world to the last great conflict, the symbols are dropped and the trumpet voice once more gives a certain sound: "Behold, I come as a thief. Blessed is he that watcheth, and keepeth his garments, lest he walk naked, and they see his shame" [Rev. 16:15]. After the transgression of Adam and Eve they were naked, for the garment of light and security had departed from them.

The world will have forgotten the admonition and warnings of God as did the inhabitants of the Noatic world, as did also the dwellers in Sodom. They awoke with all their plans and inventions of iniquity, but suddenly the shower of fire came from heaven and consumed the godless inhabitants. "Thus shall it be in the day when the Son of man is revealed" [Luke 17:30].—14MR 96, 97 (1896).

The Last Great Battle Between Good and Evil

Two great opposing powers are revealed in the last great battle. On one side stands the Creator of heaven and earth. All on His side bear His signet. They are obedient to His commands. On the other side stands the prince of darkness, with those who have chosen apostasy and rebellion.—7BC 982, 983 (1901).

A terrible conflict is before us. We are nearing the battle of the great day of God Almighty. That which has been held in control is to be let loose. The angel of mercy is folding her wings, preparing to step down from the throne and leave the world to the control of Satan. The principalities and powers of earth are in bitter revolt against the God of heaven. They are filled with hatred against those who serve Him, and soon, very soon, will be fought the last great battle between good and evil. The earth is to be the battle field—the scene of the final contest and the final victory. Here, where for so long Satan has led men against God, rebellion is to be forever suppressed.—RH May 13, 1902.

The battles waging between the two armies are as real as those fought by the armies of this world, and on the issue of the spiritual conflict eternal destinies depend.—PK 176 (c. 1914).

All the World Will Be Gathered on One Side or the Other

All the world will be on one side or the other of the question. The battle of Armageddon will be fought. And that day must find none of us sleeping. Wide awake we must be, as wise virgins having oil in our vessels with our lamps. The power of the Holy Ghost must be upon us and the Captain of the Lord's host will stand at the head of the angels of heaven to direct the battle.—3 SM 426 (1890).

The enmity of Satan against good will be manifested more and more as he brings his forces into activity in his last work of rebellion, and every soul that is not fully surrendered to God and kept by divine power will form an alliance with Satan against heaven and join in battle against the Ruler of the universe.—TM 465 (1892).

Soon all the inhabitants of the earth will have taken sides, either for or against the government of heaven.—7T 141 (1902).

The Seventh Plague

We need to study the pouring out of the seventh vial [Rev. 16:17-21]. The powers of evil will not yield up the conflict without a struggle. But Providence has a part to act in the battle of Armageddon. When the earth is lighted with the glory of the angel of Revelation eighteen, the religious elements, good and evil, will awake from slumber, and the armies of the living God will take the field.—7BC 983 (1899).

The battle of Armageddon is soon to be fought. He on whose vesture is written the name, King of kings and Lord of lords, leads forth the armies of heaven on white horses, clothed in fine linen, clean and white [Rev. 19:11-16].—7BC 982 (1899).

The whole earth heaves and swells like the waves of the sea. Its surface is breaking up. Its very foundations seem to be giving way. Mountain chains are sinking. Inhabited islands disappear. The seaports that have become like Sodom for wickedness, are swallowed up by the angry waters. . . . The proudest cities of the earth are laid low. The lordly palaces, upon which the world's great men have lavished their wealth in order to glorify themselves, are crumbling to ruin before their eyes. Prison walls are rent asunder, and God's people, who have been held in bondage for their faith, are set free.—GC 637 (1911).

18.

The Seven Last Plagues and the Righteous

(The Great Time of Trouble, Part 2)

The Great Time of Trouble Begins After Probation's Close

When Christ shall cease His work as mediator in man's behalf, then this time of trouble will begin. Then the case of every soul will have been decided, and there will be no atoning blood to cleanse from sin. When Jesus leaves His position as man's intercessor before God the solemn announcement is made, "He that is unjust, let him be unjust still: and he which is filthy, let him be filthy still: and he that is righteous, let him be righteous still: and he that is holy, let him be holy still" (Rev. 22:11). Then the restraining Spirit of God is withdrawn from the earth.—PP 201 (1890).

God's People Are Prepared for the Trying Hour Before Them

When the third angel's message closes, mercy no longer pleads for the guilty inhabitants of the earth.

The people of God have accomplished their work. They have received "the latter rain," "the refreshing from the presence of the Lord," and they are prepared for the trying hour before them.

Angels are hastening to and fro in heaven. An angel returning from the earth announces that his work is done; the final test has been brought upon the world, and all who have proved themselves loyal to the divine precepts have received "the seal of the living God." Then Jesus ceases His intercession in the sanctuary above. . . . Christ has made the atonement for His people, and blotted out their sins. The number of His subjects is made up; "the kingdom and dominion, and the greatness of the kingdom under the whole heaven," is about to be given to the heirs of salvation, and Jesus is to reign as King of kings, and Lord of lords.—GC 613, 614 (1911).

Terrible Beyond Comprehension

The season of distress and anguish before us will require a faith that can endure weariness, delay, and hunger—a faith that will not faint, though severely tried. . . .

The "time of trouble such as never was," is soon to open upon us; and we shall need an experience which we do not now possess, and which many are too indolent to obtain. It is often the case that trouble is greater in anticipation than in reality; but this is not true of the crisis before us. The most vivid presentation cannot reach the magnitude of the ordeal.—GC 621, 622 (1911).

When Jesus leaves the most holy His restraining Spirit is withdrawn from rulers and people. They are left to the control of evil angels. Then such laws will be made by the counsel and direction of Satan that, unless time should be very short, no flesh could be saved.—1T 204 (1859).

Many Laid to Rest Before Time of Trouble

It is not always safe to ask for unconditional healing. . . . He knows whether or not those for whom petitions are offered would be able to endure the trial and test that would come upon them if they lived. He knows the end from the beginning. Many will be laid away to sleep before the fiery ordeal of the time of trouble shall come upon our world.—CH 375 (1897).

The Lord has often instructed me that many little ones are to be laid away before the time of trouble. We shall see our children again. We shall meet them and know them in the heavenly courts.—2SM 259 (1899).

Satan's Goal: Destroy All Sabbathkeepers

Says the great deceiver: . . . "Our principal concern is to silence this sect of Sabbathkeepers. . . . We will finally have a law to exterminate all who will not submit to our authority."—TM 472, 473 (1884).

It is the purpose of Satan to cause them to be blotted from the earth in order that his supremacy of the world may not be disputed.—TM 37 (1893).

The remnant church will be brought into great trial and distress. Those who keep the commandments of God and the faith of Jesus will feel the ire of the dragon and his hosts. Satan numbers the world as his subjects. He has gained control of the apostate churches; but here is a little company that are resisting his supremacy. If he could blot them from the earth, his triumph would be complete. As he influenced the heathen nations to destroy Israel, so in the near future he will stir up the wicked powers of earth to destroy the people of God.—9T 231 (1909).

Arguments Used Against God's People

I saw that the four angels would hold the four winds until Jesus' work was done in the sanctuary, and then will come the seven last plagues. These plagues enraged the wicked against the righteous; they thought that we had brought the judgments of God upon them, and that if they could rid the earth of us, the plagues would then be stayed.—EW 36 (1851).

When the angel of mercy folds her wings and departs Satan will do the evil deeds he has long wished to do. Storm and tempest, war and bloodshed—in these things he delights, and thus he gathers in his harvest. And so completely will men be deceived by him that they will declare that these calamities are the result of the desecration of the first day of the week. From the pulpits of the popular churches will be heard the statement that the world is being punished because Sunday is not honored as it should be.—RH Sept. 17, 1901.

It will be urged that the few who stand in opposition to an institution of the church and a law of the state, ought not to be tolerated; that it is better for them to suffer than for whole nations to be thrown into confusion and lawlessness. The same argument eighteen hundred years ago was brought against Christ by the "rulers of the people." . . . This argument will appear conclusive.—GC 615 (1911).

Death for All Who Do Not Honor Sunday

A decree went forth to slay the saints, which caused them to cry day and night for deliverance.—EW 36, 37 (1851).

As Nebuchadnezzar the king of Babylon issued a decree that all who would not bow down and worship this image should be killed, so a proclamation will be made that all who will not reverence the Sunday institution will be punished with imprisonment and death. . . . Let all read carefully the thirteenth chapter of Revelation, for it concerns every human agent, great and small.—14MR 91 (1896).

The time of trouble is about to come upon the people of God. Then it is that the decree will go forth forbidding those who keep the Sabbath of the Lord to buy or sell, and threatening them with punishment, and even death, if they do not observe the first day of the week as the Sabbath.—HP 344 (1908).

The powers of earth, uniting to war against the commandments of God, will decree that "all, both small and great, rich and poor, free and bond" (Rev. 13:16), shall conform to the customs of the church by the observance of the false sabbath. All who refuse compliance will be visited with civil penalties, and it will finally be declared that they are deserving of death.—GC 604 (1911).

Especially will the wrath of man be aroused against those who hallow the Sabbath of the fourth commandment, and at last a universal decree will denounce these as deserving of death.—PK 512 (c. 1914).

Death Decree Similar
to That Issued by Ahasuerus

The decree that will finally go forth against the remnant people of God will be very similar to that issued by Ahasuerus against the Jews. Today the enemies of the true church see in the little company keeping the Sabbath commandment, a Mordecai at the gate. The reverence of God's people for His law is a constant rebuke to those who have cast off the fear of the Lord and are trampling on His Sabbath.—PK 605 (c. 1914).

I saw the leading men of the earth consulting together, and Satan and his angels busy around them. I saw a writing, copies of which were scattered in different parts of the land, giving orders that unless the saints should yield their peculiar faith, give up the Sabbath, and observe the first day of the week, the people were at liberty after a certain time, to put them to death.—EW 282, 283 (1858).

If the people of God will put their trust in Him and by faith rely upon His power, the devices of Satan will be defeated in our time as signally as in the days of Mordecai.—ST Feb. 22, 1910.

The Remnant Make God Their Defense

"And at that time shall Michael stand up, the great Prince which standeth for the children of thy people: and there shall be a time of trouble, such as never was since there was a nation even to that same time: and at that time thy people shall be delivered, every one that shall be found written in the book" [Dan. 12:1]. When this time of trouble comes, every case is decided; there is no longer probation, no longer mercy for the impenitent. The seal of the living God is upon His people.

This small remnant, unable to defend themselves in the deadly conflict with the powers of earth that are marshaled by the dragon host, make God their defense. The decree has been passed by the highest earthly authority that they shall worship the beast and receive his mark under pain of persecution and death. May God help His people now, for what can they then do in such a fearful conflict without His assistance!—5T 212, 213 (1882).

God's People Flee the Cities; Many Imprisoned

As the decree issued by the various rulers of Christendom against commandment keepers shall withdraw the protection of government, and abandon them to those who desire their destruction, the people of God will flee from the cities and villages and associate together in companies, dwelling in the most desolate and solitary places. Many will find refuge in the strongholds of the mountains. . . . But many of all nations and of all classes, high and low, rich and poor, black and white, will be cast into the most unjust and cruel bondage. The beloved of God pass weary days bound in chains, shut in by prison bars, sentenced to be slain, some apparently left to die of starvation in dark and loathsome dungeons.—GC 626 (1911).

Though a general decree has fixed the time when commandment keepers may be put to death, their enemies will in some cases anticipate the decree, and before the time specified, will endeavor to take their lives. But none can pass the mighty guardians stationed about every faithful soul. Some are assailed in their flight from the cities and villages; but the swords raised against them break and fall powerless as a straw. Others are defended by angels in the form of men of war.—GC 631 (1911).

The people of God are not at this time all in one place. They are in different companies and in all parts of the earth; and they will be tried singly, not in groups. Every one must stand the test for himself. —4BC 1143 (1908).

The faith of individual members of the church will be tested as though there were not another person in the world.—7BC 983 (1890).

Houses and Lands of No Use

Houses and lands will be of no use to the saints in the time of trouble, for they will then have to flee before infuriated mobs, and at that time their possessions cannot be disposed of to advance the cause of present truth. . . .

I saw that if any held on to their property, and did not inquire of the Lord as to their duty, He would not make duty known, and they would be permitted to keep their property, and in the time of trouble it would come up before them like a mountain to crush them, and they would try to dispose of it, but would not be able. . . . But if they desired to be taught, He would teach them, in a time of need, when to sell and how much to sell.—EW 56, 57 (1851).

It is too late now to cling to worldly treasures. Soon unnecessary houses and lands will be of no benefit to anyone, for the curse of God will rest more and more heavily upon the earth. The call comes, "Sell that ye have, and give alms" [Luke 12:33]. This message should be faithfully borne—urged home to the hearts of the people—that God's own property may be returned to Him in offerings to advance His work in the world.—16MR 348 (1901).

Like the Time of Jacob's Trouble

A decree will finally be issued against those who hallow the Sabbath of the fourth commandment,

denouncing them as deserving of the severest punishment, and giving the people liberty, after a certain
time, to put them to death. Romanism in the Old
World, and apostate Protestantism in the New, will
pursue a similar course toward those who honor all
the divine precepts. The people of God will then be
plunged into those scenes of affliction and distress
described by the prophet as the time of Jacob's
trouble.—GC 615, 616 (1911).

To human sight it will appear that the people of
God must soon seal their testimony with their blood,
as did the martyrs before them. They themselves
begin to fear that the Lord has left them to fall by the
hand of their enemies. It is a time of fearful agony. Day
and night they cry unto God for deliverance. . . . Like
Jacob, all are wrestling with God. Their countenances
express their internal struggle. Paleness sits upon
every face. Yet they cease not their earnest intercession.—GC 630 (1911).

Jacob's experience during that night of wrestling
and anguish represents the trial through which the
people of God must pass just before Christ's second
coming. The prophet Jeremiah, in holy vision looking
down to this time, said, "We have heard a voice of
trembling, of fear, and not of peace. . . . All faces are
turned into paleness. Alas! for that day is great, so
that none is like it: it is even the time of Jacob's
trouble; but he shall be saved out of it" (Jer. 30:5-7).
—PP 201 (1890).

The Righteous Have No Concealed Wrongs to Reveal

In the time of trouble, if the people of God had unconfessed sins to appear before them while tortured with fear and anguish, they would be overwhelmed; despair would cut off their faith, and they could not have confidence to plead with God for deliverance. But while they have a deep sense of their unworthiness, they have no concealed wrongs to reveal. Their sins have gone beforehand to judgment, and have been blotted out; and they cannot bring them to remembrance.—GC 620 (1911).

God's people . . . will have a deep sense of their shortcomings, and as they review their lives their hopes will sink. But remembering the greatness of God's mercy, and their own sincere repentance, they will plead His promises made through Christ to helpless, repenting sinners. Their faith will not fail because their prayers are not immediately answered. They will lay hold of the strength of God, as Jacob laid hold of the Angel, and the language of their souls will be, "I will not let Thee go, except Thou bless me."—PP 202 (1890).

The Saints Will Not Lose Their Lives

God would not suffer the wicked to destroy those who were expecting translation, and who would not bow to the decree of the beast or receive his mark. I saw that if the wicked were permitted to slay the saints, Satan and all his evil host, and all who hate

God, would be gratified. And oh, what a triumph it would be for his satanic majesty, to have power, in the last closing struggle, over those who had so long waited to behold Him whom they loved! Those who have mocked at the idea of the saints' going up will witness the care of God for His people, and behold their glorious deliverance.—EW 284 (1858).

The people of God will not be free from suffering; but while persecuted and distressed, while they endure privation, and suffer for want of food, they will not be left to perish.—GC 629 (1911).

If the blood of Christ's faithful witnesses were shed at this time, it would not, like the blood of the martyrs, be as seed sown to yield a harvest for God.—GC 634 (1911).

God Will Provide

The Lord has shown me repeatedly that it is contrary to the Bible to make any provision for our temporal wants in the time of trouble. I saw that if the saints had food laid up by them or in the field in the time of trouble, when sword, famine, and pestilence are in the land, it would be taken from them by violent hands, and strangers would reap their fields.

Then will be the time for us to trust wholly in God, and He will sustain us. I saw that our bread and water will be sure at that time, and that we shall not lack or suffer hunger, for God is able to spread a table for us in the wilderness. If necessary He would send ravens to feed us, as He did to feed Elijah, or rain manna from heaven, as He did for the Israelites.—EW 56 (1851).

I saw that a time of trouble was before us, when stern necessity will compel the people of God to live on bread and water. . . . In the time of trouble none will labor with their hands. Their sufferings will be mental, and God will provide food for them.—Ms 2, 1858.

The time of trouble is just before us, and then stern necessity will require the people of God to deny self and to eat merely enough to sustain life, but God will prepare us for that time. In that fearful hour our necessity will be God's opportunity to impart His strengthening power and to sustain His people.—1T 206 (1859).

Bread and water is all that is promised to the remnant in the time of trouble.—SR 129 (1870).

In the time of trouble, just before the coming of Christ, the righteous will be preserved through the ministration of heavenly angels.—PP 256 (1890).

No Intercessor, but Constant Communion With Christ

Christ has made the atonement for His people and blotted out their sins. The number of His subjects is made up. . . .

When He leaves the sanctuary, darkness covers the inhabitants of the earth. In that fearful time the

righteous must live in the sight of a holy God without
an intercessor.—GC 613, 614 (1911).

Will the Lord forget His people in this trying hour?
. . . Though enemies may thrust them into prison, yet
dungeon walls cannot cut off the communication
between their souls and Christ. One who sees their
every weakness, who is acquainted with every trial, is
above all earthly powers, and angels will come to them
in lonely cells, bringing light and peace from heaven.
The prison will be as a palace, for the rich in faith
dwell there, and the gloomy walls will be lighted up
with heavenly light as when Paul and Silas prayed
and sang praises at midnight in the Philippian dungeon.—GC 626, 627 (1911).

Could men see with heavenly vision, they would
behold companies of angels that excel in strength stationed about those who have kept the word of Christ's
patience. With sympathizing tenderness, angels have
witnessed their distress and have heard their prayers.
They are waiting the word of their Commander to snatch
them from their peril. . . . The precious Saviour will send
help just when we need it.—GC 630, 633 (1911).

It is impossible to give any idea of the experience of
the people of God who shall be alive upon the earth
when celestial glory and a repetition of the persecutions of the past are blended. They will walk in the
light proceeding from the throne of God. By means of
the angels there will be constant communication
between heaven and earth. . . .

In the midst of the time of trouble that is coming—a time of trouble such as has not been since there was a nation—God's chosen people will stand unmoved. Satan and his host cannot destroy them, for angels that excel in strength will protect them.—9T 16, 17 (1909).

God's People Cherish No Sinful Desires

Now, while our great High Priest is making the atonement for us, we should seek to become perfect in Christ. Not even by a thought could our Saviour be brought to yield to the power of temptation. Satan finds in human hearts some point where he can gain a foothold; some sinful desire is cherished, by means of which his temptations assert their power. But Christ declared of Himself: "The prince of this world cometh, and hath nothing in Me" (John 14:30). Satan could find nothing in the Son of God that would enable him to gain the victory. He had kept His Father's commandments, and there was no sin in Him that Satan could use to his advantage. This is the condition in which those must be found who shall stand in the time of trouble.—GC 623 (1911).

The Battle Against Self Continues

So long as Satan reigns, we shall have self to subdue, besetting sins to overcome; so long as life shall last, there will be no stopping place, no point which we can reach and say, I have fully attained. Sanctification is the result of lifelong obedience.—AA 560, 561 (1911).

Constant war against the carnal mind must be maintained; and we must be aided by the refining influence of the grace of God, which will attract the mind upward and habituate it to meditate upon pure and holy things.—2T 479 (1870).

We may create an unreal world in our own mind or picture an ideal church, where the temptations of Satan no longer prompt to evil; but perfection exists only in our imagination.—RH Aug. 8, 1893.

When human beings receive holy flesh, they will not remain on the earth, but will be taken to heaven. While sin is forgiven in this life, its results are not now wholly removed. It is at His coming that Christ is to "change our vile body, that it may be fashioned like unto His glorious body."—2SM 33 (1901).

The 144,000

They sing "a new song" before the throne, a song which no man can learn save the hundred and forty and four thousand. It is the song of Moses and the Lamb—a song of deliverance. None but the hundred and forty-four thousand can learn that song, for it is the song of their experience—an experience such as no other company have ever had. "These are they which follow the Lamb whithersoever He goeth." These, having been translated from the earth, from among the living, are counted as "the first fruits unto God and to the Lamb" (Rev. 15:2, 3; 14:1-5). "These are they which came out of great tribulation"; they have passed through the time of trouble such as never was since there was a nation; they have endured the anguish of the time of Jacob's trouble; they have stood without an intercessor through the final outpouring of God's judgments.—GC 648, 649 (1911).

It is not His will that they shall get into controversy over questions which will not help them spiritually, such as, Who is to compose the hundred and forty-four thousand? This those who are the elect of God will in a short time know without question.—1SM 174 (1901).

God's People Delivered

Satan's host and wicked men will surround them and exult over them because there will seem to be no way of escape for them. But in the midst of their revelry and triumph there is heard peal upon peal of the loudest thunder. The heavens have gathered blackness, and are only illuminated by the blazing light and terrible glory from heaven, as God utters His voice from His holy habitation.

The foundations of the earth shake, buildings totter and fall with a terrible crash. The sea boils like a pot and the whole earth is in terrible commotion. The captivity of the righteous is turned, and with sweet and solemn whisperings they say to one another: "We are delivered. It is the voice of God."—1T 353, 354 (1862).

When the protection of human laws shall be withdrawn from those who honor the law of God, there will be, in different lands, a simultaneous movement for their destruction. As the time appointed in the decree draws near, the people will conspire to root out the hated sect. It will be determined to strike in one night a decisive blow, which shall utterly silence the voice of dissent and reproof.

The people of God—some in prison cells, some hidden in solitary retreats in the forests and the mountains—still plead for divine protection, while in every quarter companies of armed men, urged on by hosts of evil angels, are preparing for the work of death. . . . With shouts of triumph, jeering, and imprecation, throngs of evil men are about to rush upon their prey when, lo, a dense blackness, deeper than the darkness of the night, falls upon the earth. . . .

It is at midnight that God manifests His power for the deliverance of His people. . . . In the midst of the angry heavens is one clear space of indescribable glory, whence comes the voice of God like the sound of many waters, saying, "It is done" (Rev. 16:17). That voice shakes the heavens and the earth. . . .

The proudest cities of the earth are laid low. The lordly palaces, upon which the world's great men have lavished their wealth in order to glorify themselves, are crumbling to ruin before their eyes. Prison walls are rent asunder, and God's people, who have been held in bondage for their faith, are set free.—GC 635-637 (1911).

19.

Christ's Return

The Seventh Plague
and the Special Resurrection

There is a mighty earthquake, "such as was not since men were upon the earth, so mighty an earthquake, and so great" (Rev. 16:17, 18). The firmament appears to open and shut. The glory from the throne of God seems flashing through. The mountains shake like a reed in the wind, and ragged rocks are scattered on every side. . . . The whole earth heaves and swells like the waves of the sea. Its surface is breaking up. Its very foundations seem to be giving way. Mountain chains are sinking. Inhabited islands disappear. The seaports that have become like Sodom for wickedness are swallowed up by the angry waters. . . . Great hailstones, every one "about the weight of a talent," are doing their work of destruction (verses 19, 21) . . . .

Graves are opened, and "many of them that sleep in the dust of the earth . . . awake, some to everlasting life, and some to shame and everlasting contempt" (Dan. 12:2). All who have died in the faith of the third angel's message come forth from the tomb glorified to hear God's covenant of peace with those who have kept His law. "They also which pierced Him" (Rev. 1:7), those that mocked and derided Christ's dying agonies, and the most violent opposers of His truth and His people, are raised to behold Him in His glory, and to see the honor placed upon the loyal and obedient.—GC 636, 637 (1911).

God Announces the Time of Christ's Coming

Dark, heavy clouds came up and clashed against each other. The atmosphere parted and rolled back. Then we could look up through the open space in Orion, whence came the voice of God.—EW 41 (1851).

Soon we heard the voice of God[1] like many waters, which gave us the day and hour of Jesus' coming. The living saints, 144,000 in number, knew and understood the voice, while the wicked thought it was thunder and an earthquake.—EW 15 (1851).

As God spoke the day and the hour of Jesus' coming, and delivered the everlasting covenant to His people, He spoke one sentence, and then paused, while the words were rolling through the earth. The Israel of God stood with their eyes fixed upward, listening to the words as they came from the mouth of Jehovah and rolled through the earth like peals of loudest thunder. It was awfully solemn. At the end of every sentence the saints shouted, "Glory! Hallelujah!" Their

---

1. The voice of God is heard repeatedly during the period immediately preceding Christ's return. See *The Great Controversy*, pp. 632, 633, 636, 638, 640, 641.

countenances were lighted up with the glory of God, and they shone with glory as did the face of Moses when he came down from Sinai. The wicked could not look upon them for the glory. And when the never-ending blessing was pronounced on those who had honored God in keeping His Sabbath holy, there was a mighty shout of victory over the beast and over his image.—EW 285, 286 (1858).

I have not the slightest knowledge as to the time spoken by the voice of God. I heard the hour proclaimed, but had no remembrance of that hour after I came out of vision. Scenes of such thrilling, solemn interest passed before me as no language is adequate to describe. It was all a living reality to me, for close upon this scene appeared the great white cloud, upon which was seated the Son of man.—1SM 76 (1888).

The Terror of the Lost

When the earth is reeling to and fro like a drunkard, when the heavens are shaking and the great day of the Lord has come, who shall be able to stand? One object they behold in trembling agony from which they will try in vain to escape. "Behold, He cometh with clouds; and every eye shall see Him" (Rev. 1:7). The unsaved utter wild imprecations to dumb nature—their god: "Mountains and rocks, fall on us, and hide us from the face of Him that sitteth on the throne" (Rev. 6:16).—TMK 356 (1896).

When the voice of God turns the captivity of His people, there is a terrible awakening of those who have

lost all in the great conflict of life. . . . The gain of a
lifetime is swept away in a moment. The rich bemoan
the destruction of their grand houses, the scattering of
their gold and silver. . . . The wicked are filled with
regret, not because of their sinful neglect of God and
their fellow men, but because God has conquered.
They lament that the result is what it is, but they do
not repent of their wickedness.—GC 654 (1911).

Jesus Descends in Power and Glory

Soon there appears in the east a small black cloud,
about half the size of a man's hand. It is the cloud
which surrounds the Saviour, and which seems in the
distance to be shrouded in darkness. The people of
God know this to be the sign of the Son of man. In
solemn silence they gaze upon it as it draws nearer the
earth, becoming lighter and more glorious, until it is
a great white cloud, its base a glory like consuming
fire, and above it the rainbow of the covenant. Jesus
rides forth as a mighty conqueror. . . .

With anthems of celestial melody the holy angels,
a vast, unnumbered throng, attend Him on His way.
The firmament seems filled with radiant forms—"ten
thousand times ten thousand, and thousands of thousands." No human pen can portray the scene, no
mortal mind is adequate to conceive its splendor. . . .

The King of kings descends upon the cloud, wrapped
in flaming fire. The heavens are rolled together as a
scroll, the earth trembles before Him, and every
mountain and island is moved out of its place.—GC
640-642 (1911).

The Reaction of Those Who Pierced Him

Those who have acted the most prominent part in the rejection and crucifixion of Christ come forth to see Him as He is, and those who have rejected Christ come up and see the saints glorified, and it is at that time that the saints are changed in a moment, in the twinkling of an eye, and are caught up to meet their Lord in the air. The very ones who placed upon Him the purple robe and put the crown of thorns upon His brow, and those who put the nails through His hands and feet, look upon Him and bewail.—9MR 252 (1886).

They remember how His love was slighted and His compassion abused. They think of how Barabbas, a murderer and a robber, was chosen in His stead, how Jesus was crowned with thorns and scourged and crucified, how in the hours of His agony on the cross the priests and rulers taunted Him, saying, "Let Him come down from the cross, and we will believe Him. He saved others, Himself He cannot save." All the insult and despite offered to Christ, all the suffering caused to His disciples, will be as fresh in their recollection as when the satanic deeds were done.

The voice which they heard so often in entreaty and persuasion will again sound in their ears. Every tone of gracious solicitation will vibrate as distinctly in their ears as when the Saviour spoke in the synagogues and on the street. Then those who pierced Him will call on the rocks and mountains to fall on them and hide them from the face of Him that sitteth on the throne and from the wrath of the Lamb.—Letter 131, 1900.

"Awake, Ye That Sleep, and Arise!"

The clouds begin to roll back like a scroll and there is the bright, clear sign of the Son of man. The children of God know what that cloud means. The sound of music is heard, and as it nears, the graves are opened and the dead are raised.—9MR 251, 252 (1886).

"Marvel not at this: for the hour is coming, in the which all that are in the graves shall hear his voice, and shall come forth" [John 5:28, 29]. This voice is soon to resound through all the nations of the dead, and every saint who sleeps in Jesus shall awake and leave his prison house.—Ms 137, 1897.

The precious dead, from Adam down to the last saint who dies, will hear the voice of the Son of God and will come forth from the grave to immortal life. —DA 606 (1898).

Amid the reeling of the earth, the flash of lightning, and the roar of thunder, the voice of the Son of God calls forth the sleeping saints. He looks upon the graves of the righteous, then, raising His hands to heaven, He cries: "Awake, awake, awake, ye that sleep in the dust, and arise!" Throughout the length and breadth of the earth the dead shall hear that voice, and they that hear shall live. And the whole earth shall ring with the tread of the exceeding great army of every nation, kindred, tongue, and people. From the prison house of death they come, clothed with immortal glory, crying: "O death, where is thy sting? O grave, where is thy victory?" (1 Cor. 15:55).

And the living righteous and the risen saints unite their voices in a long, glad shout of victory.—GC 644 (1911).

From Caves and Dens and Dungeons

In the fastnesses of the mountains, in the caves and dens of the earth, the Saviour reveals His presence and His glory.

Yet a little while, and He that is to come will come and will not tarry. His eyes as a flame of fire penetrate into the fast-closed dungeons and hunt out the hidden ones, for their names are written in the Lamb's book of life. The eyes of the Saviour are above us, around us, noting every difficulty, discerning every danger; and there is no place where His eyes cannot penetrate, no sorrows and sufferings of His people where the sympathy of Christ does not reach. . . .

The child of God will be terror-stricken at the first sight of the majesty of Jesus Christ. He feels that he cannot live in His holy presence. But the word comes to him as to John, "Fear not." Jesus laid His right hand upon John; He raised him up from his prostrate position. So will He do unto His loyal, trusting ones. —TMK 360, 361 (1886).

The heirs of God have come from garrets, from hovels, from dungeons, from scaffolds, from mountains, from deserts, from the caves of the earth, from the caverns of the sea.—GC 650 (1911).

From Ocean Depths and Mines and Mountains

When Christ comes to gather to Himself those who

have been faithful, the last trump will sound, and the whole earth, from the summits of the loftiest mountains to the lowest recesses of the deepest mines, will hear. The righteous dead will hear the sound of the last trump, and will come forth from their graves, to be clothed with immortality and to meet their Lord. —7BC 909 (1904).

I dwell with pleasure upon the resurrection of the just, who shall come forth from all parts of the earth, from rocky caverns, from dungeons, from caves of the earth, from the waters of the deep. Not one is overlooked. Every one shall hear His voice. They will come forth with triumph and victory.—Letter 113, 1886.

What a scene will these mountains and hills [in Switzerland] present when Christ, the Lifegiver, shall call forth the dead! They will come from caverns, from dungeons, from deep wells, where their bodies have been buried.—Letter 97, 1886.

The Wicked Are Slain

In the mad strife of their own fierce passions, and by the awful outpouring of God's unmingled wrath, fall the wicked inhabitants of the earth—priests, rulers, and people, rich and poor, high and low. "And the slain of the Lord shall be at that day from one end of the earth even unto the other end of the earth: they shall not be lamented, neither gathered, nor buried" (Jer. 25:33).

At the coming of Christ the wicked are blotted from the face of the whole earth—consumed with the spirit of

His mouth and destroyed by the brightness of His glory. Christ takes His people to the city of God, and the earth is emptied of its inhabitants.—GC 657 (1911).

To sin, wherever found, "our God is a consuming fire" (Heb. 12:29). In all who submit to His power the Spirit of God will consume sin. But if men cling to sin, they become identified with it. Then the glory of God, which destroys sin, must destroy them.—DA 107 (1898).

The glory of His countenance, which to the righteous is life, will be to the wicked a consuming fire. —DA 600 (1898).

Destruction of the Wicked an Act of Mercy

Could those whose hearts are filled with hatred of God, of truth and holiness, mingle with the heavenly throng and join their songs of praise? Could they endure the glory of God and the Lamb? No, no; years of probation were granted them, that they might form characters for heaven; but they have never trained the mind to love purity; they have never learned the language of heaven, and now it is too late. A life of rebellion against God has unfitted them for heaven. Its purity, holiness, and peace would be torture to them; the glory of God would be a consuming fire. They would long to flee from that holy place. They would welcome destruction, that they might be hidden from the face of Him who died to redeem them. The destiny of the wicked is fixed by their own choice. Their exclusion from heaven is voluntary with themselves, and just and merciful on the part of God.—GC 542, 543 (1911).

Homeward Bound!

The living righteous are changed "in a moment, in the twinkling of an eye." At the voice of God they were glorified; now they are made immortal, and with the risen saints are caught up to meet their Lord in the air. Angels "gather together His elect from the four winds, from one end of heaven to the other." Little children are borne by holy angels to their mothers' arms. Friends long separated by death are united, nevermore to part, and with songs of gladness ascend together to the city of God.—GC 645 (1911).

We all entered the cloud together, and were seven days ascending to the sea of glass.—EW 16 (1851).

And as the chariot rolled upward, the wheels cried, "Holy," and the wings, as they moved, cried, "Holy," and the retinue of holy angels around the cloud cried, "Holy, holy, holy, Lord God Almighty!" And the saints in the cloud cried, "Glory! Alleluia!"—EW 35 (1851).

Oh, how glorious it will be to see Him and be welcomed as His redeemed ones! Long have we waited, but our hope is not to grow dim. If we can but see the King in His beauty we shall be forever blessed. I feel as if I must cry aloud, "Homeward bound!"—8T 253 (1904).

The Angels Sing, Christ Has Conquered!

In that day the redeemed will shine forth in the glory of the Father and the Son. The angels, touching their golden harps, will welcome the King and His trophies of victory—those who have been washed and made white in the blood of the Lamb. A song of triumph will peal forth, filling all heaven. Christ has conquered. He enters the heavenly courts, accompanied by His redeemed ones, the witnesses that His mission of suffering and sacrifice has not been in vain.—9T 285, 286 (1909).

With unutterable love, Jesus welcomes His faithful ones to the joy of their Lord. The Saviour's joy is in seeing in the kingdom of glory the souls that have been saved by His agony and humiliation.—GC 647 (1911).

In the results of His work Christ will behold its recompense. In that great multitude which no man could number, presented "faultless before the presence of His glory with exceeding joy," He whose blood has redeemed and whose life has taught us "shall see of the travail of His soul, and shall be satisfied."—Ed 309 (1903).

The Saints Given Crowns and Harps

I saw a very great number of angels bring from the city glorious crowns—a crown for every saint, with his name written thereon. As Jesus called for the crowns, angels presented them to Him, and with His own right hand, the lovely Jesus placed the crowns on the heads of the saints.—EW 288 (1858).

On the sea of glass the 144,000 stood in a perfect square. Some of them had very bright crowns, others not so bright. Some crowns appeared heavy with stars, while others had but few. All were perfectly satisfied with their crowns.—EW 16, 17 (1851).

The crown of life will be bright or dim, will glitter with many stars, or be lighted by few gems, in accordance with our own course of action.—6BC 1105 (1895).

There will be no one saved in heaven with a starless crown. If you enter, there will be some soul in the courts of glory that has found an entrance there through your instrumentality.—ST June 6, 1892.

Before entering the city of God, the Saviour bestows upon His followers the emblems of victory, and invests them with the insignia of their royal state. The glittering ranks are drawn up in the form of a hollow square about their King. . . . Upon the heads of the overcomers, Jesus with His own right hand places the crown of glory. . . . In every hand are placed the victor's palm and the shining harp. Then, as the commanding angels strike the note, every hand sweeps the harp strings with skillful touch, awaking sweet music in rich, melodious strains. . . . Before the ransomed throng is the holy city. Jesus opens wide the pearly gates, and the nations that have kept the truth enter in.—GC 645, 646 (1911).

20.

The Inheritance of the Saints[1]

A Gift From the Lord

Christ, only Christ and His righteousness, will obtain for us a passport into heaven.—Letter 6b, 1890.

The proud heart strives to earn salvation, but both our title to heaven and our fitness for it are found in the righteousness of Christ.—DA 300 (1898).

That we might become members of the heavenly family, He became a member of the earthly family. —DA 638 (1898).

Better than a title to the noblest palace on earth is

---

1. The various views of heaven and the new earth presented to Ellen White were representations of eternal realities. She was shown heavenly things in terms of human concepts. Because of the limits of our human comprehension and language, we cannot fully know the actual appearance of the scenes depicted. "Now we see through a glass, darkly; but then face to face: now I know in part; but then shall I know even as also I am known" (1 Cor. 13:12).

a title to the mansions our Lord has gone to prepare. And better than all the words of earthly praise, will be the Saviour's words to His faithful servants, "Come, ye blessed of My Father, inherit the kingdom prepared for you from the foundation of the world." —COL 374 (1900).

Why We Should Think About the Future World

Jesus has brought heaven to view, and presents its glory to our eyes in order that eternity may not be dropped out of our reckoning.—ST April 4, 1895.

With eternal realities in view we will habitually cultivate thoughts of the presence of God. This will be a shield against the incoming of the enemy; it will give strength and assurance, and lift the soul above fear. Breathing in the atmosphere of heaven, we will not be breathing the malaria of the world. . . .

Jesus comes to present the advantages and beautiful imagery of the heavenly, that the attractions of heaven shall become familiar to the thoughts, and memory's hall be hung with pictures of celestial and eternal loveliness. . . .

The great Teacher gives man a view of the future world. He brings it, with its attractive possessions, within the range of his vision. . . . If He can fasten the mind upon the future life and its blessedness, in comparison with the temporal concerns of this world, the striking contrast is deeply impressed upon the mind, absorbing the heart and soul and the whole being.—OHC 285, 286 (1890).

The Christian's Motives

Motives stronger, and agencies more powerful, could never be brought into operation; the exceeding rewards for right-doing, the enjoyment of heaven, the society of the angels, the communion and love of God and His Son, the elevation and extension of all our powers throughout eternal ages—are these not mighty incentives and encouragements to urge us to give the heart's loving service to our Creator and Redeemer?—SC 21, 22 (1892).

If we can meet Jesus in peace and be saved, forever saved, we shall be the happiest of beings. Oh, to be at home at last where the wicked cease from troubling and the weary are at rest!—Letter 113, 1886.

I love to see everything that is beautiful in nature in this world. I think I would be perfectly satisfied with this earth, surrounded with the good things of God, if it were not blighted with the curse of sin. But we shall have new heavens and a new earth. John saw this in holy vision and said, "I heard a great voice out of heaven saying, Behold, the tabernacle of God is with men, and He will dwell with them, and they shall be His people, and God Himself shall be with them and be their God" [Rev. 21:3]. Oh, blessed hope, glorious prospect!—Letter 62, 1886.

A Real and Tangible Place

What a source of joy to the disciples to know that they had such a Friend in heaven to plead in their

behalf! Through the visible ascension of Christ all
their views and contemplation of heaven are changed.
Their minds had formerly dwelt upon it as a region of
unlimited space, tenanted by spirits without sub-
stance. Now heaven was connected with the thought
of Jesus, whom they had loved and reverenced above
all others, with whom they had conversed and journeyed, whom they had handled, even in His resur-
rected body. . . .

Heaven could no longer appear to them as an
indefinite, incomprehensible space, filled with intan-
gible spirits. They now looked upon it as their future
home, where mansions were being prepared for them
by their loving Redeemer.—3SP 262 (1878).

A fear of making the future inheritance seem too
material has led many to spiritualize away the very
truths which lead us to look upon it as our home.
Christ assured His disciples that He went to prepare
mansions for them in the Father's house.—GC 674,
675 (1911).

In the earth made new, the redeemed will engage in
the occupations and pleasures that brought happiness to
Adam and Eve in the beginning. The Eden life will be
lived, the life in garden and field.—PK 730, 731 (c. 1914).

Glory Indescribable

I saw the exceeding loveliness and glory of Jesus.
His countenance was brighter than the sun at noon-
day. His robe was whiter than the whitest white. How

can I . . . describe to you the glories of heaven, and the lovely angels singing and playing upon their harps of ten strings!—Letter 3, 1851.

The wonderful things I there saw I cannot describe. Oh, that I could talk in the language of Canaan, then could I tell a little of the glory of the better world.—EW 19 (1851).

Language is altogether too feeble to attempt a description of heaven. As the scene rises before me, I am lost in amazement. Carried away with the surpassing splendor and excellent glory, I lay down the pen and exclaim, "Oh, what love! what wondrous love!" The most exalted language fails to describe the glory of heaven or the matchless depths of a Saviour's love.—EW 289 (1858).

Human language is inadequate to describe the reward of the righteous. It will be known only to those who behold it. No finite mind can comprehend the glory of the Paradise of God.—GC 675 (1911).

If we could have but one view of the celestial city, we would never wish to dwell on earth again.—ST April 8, 1889.

Streams, Hills, and Trees

Here we saw the tree of life and the throne of God. Out of the throne came a pure river of water, and on either side of the river was the tree of life. On one side of the river was a trunk of a tree, and a trunk on the other side of the river, both of pure, transparent gold. At first I thought I saw two trees. I looked again, and saw that they were united at the top in one tree. So it was the tree of life on either side of the river of life. Its branches bowed to the place where we stood, and the fruit was glorious; it looked like gold mixed with silver.—EW 17 (1851).

There are ever-flowing streams, clear as crystal, and beside them waving trees cast their shadows upon the paths prepared for the ransomed of the Lord. There the wide-spreading plains swell into hills of beauty, and the mountains of God rear their lofty summits. On those peaceful plains, beside those living streams, God's people, so long pilgrims and wanderers, shall find a home.—GC 675 (1911).

Flowers, Fruit, and Animals

I saw another field full of all kinds of flowers, and as I plucked them, I cried out, "They will never fade." Next I saw a field of tall grass, most glorious to behold; it was living green and had a reflection of silver and gold, as it waved proudly to the glory of King Jesus. Then we entered a field full of all kinds of beasts—the lion, the lamb, the leopard, and the wolf, all together in perfect union. We passed through the midst of them, and they followed on peaceably after.

Then we entered a wood, not like the dark woods we have here; no, no; but light, and all over glorious; the branches of the trees moved to and fro, and we all cried out, "We will dwell safely in the wilderness and sleep in the woods." We passed through the woods, for we were on our way to Mount Zion. . . .

On the mount was a glorious temple. . . . There were all kinds of trees around the temple to beautify the place: the box, the pine, the fir, the oil, the myrtle, the pomegranate, and the fig tree bowed down with the weight of its timely figs—these made the place all over glorious. . . .

And I saw a table of pure silver; it was many miles in length, yet our eyes could extend over it. I saw the fruit of the tree of life, the manna, almonds, figs, pomegranates, grapes, and many other kinds of fruit. I asked Jesus to let me eat of the fruit.—EW 18, 19 (1851).

The Vigor of Eternal Youth

All come forth from their graves the same in stature as when they entered the tomb. Adam, who stands among the risen throng, is of lofty height and majestic form, in stature but little below the Son of God. He presents a marked contrast to the people of later generations; in this one respect is shown the great degeneracy of the race. But all arise with the freshness and vigor of eternal youth. . . . Restored to the tree of life in the long-lost Eden, the redeemed will "grow up" (Mal. 4:2) to the full stature of a race in its primeval glory.—GC 644, 645 (1911).

If Adam, at his creation, had not been endowed with twenty times as much vital force as men now have, the race, with their present habits of living in violation of natural law, would have become extinct.—3T 138 (1872).

None will need or desire repose. There will be no weariness in doing the will of God and offering praise to His name. We shall ever feel the freshness of the morning, and shall ever be far from its close. . . . The acquirement of knowledge will not weary the mind or exhaust the energies.—GC 676, 677 (1911).

Heaven is all health.—3T 172 (1872).

Happiness Guaranteed

Jesus lifted the veil from the future life. "In the resurrection," He said, "they neither marry, nor are given in marriage, but are as the angels of God in heaven" [Matt. 22:30].—DA 605 (1898).

There are men today who express their belief that there will be marriages and births in the new earth, but those who believe the Scriptures cannot accept such doctrines. The doctrine that children will be born in the new earth is not a part of the "sure word of prophecy." . . .

It is presumption to indulge in suppositions and theories regarding matters that God has not made known to us in His Word. We need not enter into speculation regarding our future state.—1SM 172, 173 (1904).

Workers for God should not spend time speculating as to what conditions will prevail in the new earth. It is presumption to indulge in suppositions and theories regarding matters that the Lord has not revealed. He has made every provision for our happiness in the future life, and we are not to speculate regarding His plans for us. Neither are we to measure the conditions of the future life by the conditions of this life.—GW 314 (1904).

Identity of the Redeemed Preserved

The resurrection of Jesus was a type of the final resurrection of all who sleep in Him. The countenance of the risen Saviour, His manner, His speech, were all familiar to His disciples. As Jesus arose from the dead, so those who sleep in Him are to rise again. We shall know our friends, even as the disciples knew Jesus. They may have been deformed, diseased, or disfigured in this mortal life, and they rise in perfect health and symmetry, yet in the glorified body their identity will be perfectly preserved.—DA 804 (1898).

The same form will come forth, but it will be free from disease and every defect. It lives again, bearing the same individuality of features, so that friend will recognize friend.—6BC 1093 (1900).

There we shall know even as also we are known. There the loves and sympathies that God has planted in the soul will find truest and sweetest exercise.—Ed 306 (1903).

A Ruddy Complexion and a Robe of Light

As Adam came forth from the hand of his Creator, he was of noble height, and of beautiful symmetry. He was more than twice as tall as men now living upon earth, and was well proportioned. His features were perfect and beautiful. His complexion was neither white, nor sallow, but ruddy, glowing with the rich tint of health. Eve was not quite as tall as Adam. Her head reached a little above his shoulders. She, too, was noble—perfect in symmetry, and very beautiful.—3SG 34 (1864).

The sinless pair wore no artificial garments; they were clothed with a covering of light and glory, such as the angels wear. So long as they lived in obedience to God, this robe of light continued to enshroud them.—PP 45 (1890).

The Joy of Seeing Our Family in Heaven

We see a retinue of angels on either side of the gate, and as we pass in Jesus speaks, "Come, ye blessed of My Father, inherit the kingdom that is prepared for you from the foundation of the world." Here He tells you to be a partaker of His joy, and what is that? It is the joy of seeing of the travail of your soul, fathers. It is the joy of seeing that your efforts, mothers, are rewarded. Here are your children; the crown of life is upon their heads.—CG 567, 568 (1895).

God's greatest gift is Christ, whose life is ours, given for us. He died for us, and was raised for us, that we might come forth from the tomb to a glorious companionship with heavenly angels, to meet our loved ones and to recognize their faces, for the Christlikeness does not destroy their image, but transforms it into His glorious image. Every saint connected in family relationship here will know each other there.—3SM 316 (1898).

The Salvation of Infants and Imbeciles

As the little infants come forth immortal from their dusty beds, they immediately wing their way to their mother's arms. They meet again nevermore to part. But many of the little ones have no mother there. We listen in vain for the rapturous song of triumph from the mother. The angels receive the motherless infants and conduct them to the tree of life.—2SM 260 (1858).

Some questioned whether the little children of even believing parents should be saved, because they have had no test of character and all must be tested and their character determined by trial. The question is asked, "How can little children have this test and trial?" I answer that the faith of the believing parents covers the children, as when God sent His judgments upon the first-born of the Egyptians. . . .

Whether all the children of unbelieving parents will be saved we cannot tell, because God has not made known His purpose in regard to this matter, and we had better leave it where God has left it and dwell upon subjects made plain in His Word.—3SM 313-315 (1885).

In regard to the case of A, you see him as he now is and deplore his simplicity. He is without the consciousness of sin. The grace of God will remove all this hereditary, transmitted imbecility, and he will have an inheritance among the saints in light. To you the Lord has given reason. A is a child as far as the capacity of reason is concerned, but he has the submission and obedience of a child.—8MR 210 (1893).

Tribute to Faithful Mothers

When the judgment shall sit, and the books shall be opened; when the "well done" of the great Judge is pronounced, and the crown of immortal glory is placed upon the brow of the victor, many will raise their crowns in sight of the assembled universe and, pointing to their mother, say, "She made me all I am through the grace of God. Her instruction, her prayers, have been blessed to my eternal salvation."—MYP 330 (1881).

The angels of God immortalize the names of the mothers whose efforts have won their children to Jesus Christ.—CG 568 (1895).

The Reward of the Winner of Souls

When the redeemed stand before God, precious souls will respond to their names who are there because of the faithful, patient efforts put forth in their behalf, the entreaties and earnest persuasions to flee to the Stronghold. Thus those who in this world have been laborers together with God will receive their reward.—8T 196, 197 (1904).

When the gates of that beautiful city on high are swung back on their glittering hinges, and the nations that have kept the truth shall enter in, crowns of glory will be placed on their heads, and they will ascribe honor and glory and majesty to God. And at that time some will come to you, and will say, "If it had not been for the words you spoke to me in kindness, if it had not been for your tears and supplications and earnest efforts, I should never have seen the King in His beauty." What a reward is this! How insignificant is the praise of human beings in this earthly, transient life, in comparison with the infinite rewards that await the faithful in the future, immortal life!—*Words of Encouragement to Self-supporting Workers* (Ph113) 16 (1909).

Our Dispositions Unchanged

If you would be a saint in heaven you must first be a saint on earth. The traits of character you cherish in life will not be changed by death or by the resurrection. You will come up from the grave with the same disposition you manifested in your home and in society. Jesus does not change the character at His coming. The work of transformation must be done now. Our daily lives are determining our destiny. Defects of character must be repented of and overcome through the grace of Christ, and a symmetrical character must be formed while in this probationary state, that we may be fitted for the mansions above.—13MR 82 (1891).

Heaven's Peaceful and Loving Atmosphere

The peace and harmony of the heavenly courts will not be marred by the presence of one who is rough or unkind.—8T 140 (1904).

Everything in heaven is noble and elevated. All seek the interest and happiness of others. No one devotes himself to looking out and caring for self. It is the chief joy of all holy beings to witness the joy and happiness of those around them.—2T 239 (1869).

I seemed to be there where all was peace, where no stormy conflicts of earth could ever come—heaven, a kingdom of righteousness where all the holy and pure and blest are congregated, ten thousand times ten thousand and thousands of thousands, living and walking in happy, pure intimacy, praising God and the Lamb who sitteth on the throne.

Their voices were in perfect harmony. They never do each other wrong. Princes of heaven, the potentates of this mighty realm, are rivals only in good, seeking the happiness and joy of each other. The greatest there is least in self-esteem, and the least is greatest in his gratitude and wealth of love.

There are no dark errors to cloud the intellect. Truth and knowledge, clear, strong, and perfect, have chased every doubt away, and no gloom of doubt casts its baleful shadow upon its happy inhabitants. No voices of contention mar the sweet and perfect peace of heaven. Its inhabitants know no sorrow, no grief, no tears. All is in perfect harmony, in perfect order and perfect bliss. . . .

Heaven is a home where sympathy is alive in every heart, expressed in every look. Love reigns there. There are no jarring elements, no discord or contentions or war of words.—9MR 104, 105 (1882).

No Temptation and No Sin

No tree of knowledge of good and evil will afford opportunity for temptation. No tempter is there, no possibility of wrong.—Ed 302 (1903).

I heard shouts of triumph from the angels and from the redeemed saints which sounded like ten thousand musical instruments, because they were to be no more annoyed and tempted by Satan and because the inhabitants of other worlds were delivered from his presence and his temptations.—SR 416 (1858).

Communion With the Father and the Son

The people of God are privileged to hold open communion with the Father and the Son. . . . We shall see Him face to face, without a dimming veil between.—GC 676, 677 (1911).

We shall ever dwell with and enjoy the light of His precious countenance. My heart leaps with joy at the cheering prospect!—HP 352 (1856).

Heaven is where Christ is. Heaven would not be heaven to those who love Christ, if He were not there. —Ms 41, 1897.

There will be a close and tender relationship between God and the risen saints.—DA 606 (1898).

Casting at the feet of the Redeemer the crowns that He has placed on our heads, and touching our golden harps, we shall fill all heaven with praise to Him that sitteth on the throne.—8T 254 (1904).

If, during this life, they are loyal to God, they will at last "see His face; and His name shall be in their foreheads" (Rev. 22:4). And what is the happiness of heaven but to see God? What greater joy could come to the sinner saved by the grace of Christ than to look upon the face of God and know Him as Father?—8T 268 (1904).

Fellowship With Angels and the Faithful of All Ages

Every redeemed one will understand the ministry of angels in his own life. The angel who was his guardian from his earliest moment, the angel who watched his steps and covered his head in the day of peril, the angel who was with him in the valley of the shadow of death, who marked his resting place, who was the first to greet him in the resurrection morning—what will it be to hold converse with him, and to learn the history of divine interposition in the individual life, of heavenly cooperation in every work for humanity!—Ed 305 (1903).

From what dangers, seen and unseen, we have been preserved through the interposition of the angels, we shall never know, until in the light of eternity we see the providences of God.—DA 240 (1898).

The loves and sympathies which God Himself has planted in the soul shall there find truest and sweetest exercise. The pure communion with holy beings, the harmonious social life with the blessed angels and with the faithful ones of all ages who have washed their robes and made them white in the blood of the Lamb, the sacred ties that bind together "the whole family in heaven and earth" (Eph. 3:15)—these help to constitute the happiness of the redeemed.—GC 677 (1911).

Bearing Testimony to Unfallen Beings

"The Son of man came not to be ministered unto, but to minister" [Matt. 20:28]. Christ's work below is His work above, and our reward for working with Him in this world will be the greater power and wider privilege of working with Him in the world to come. "Ye are my witnesses, saith the Lord, that I am God" [Isa. 43:12]. This also we shall be in eternity.

For what was the great controversy permitted to continue throughout the ages? Why was it that Satan's existence was not cut short at the outset of his rebellion?—It was that the universe might be convinced of God's justice in His dealing with evil; that sin might receive eternal condemnation. In the plan of redemption there are heights and depths that eternity itself can never exhaust, marvels into which the angels desire to look. The redeemed only, of all created beings, have in their own experience known the actual conflict with sin; they have wrought with Christ and, as even the angels could not do, have entered into the fellowship of His sufferings; will they have no testimony as to the science of redemption—nothing that will be of worth to unfallen beings?—Ed 308 (1903).

Praising God in Rich, Melodious Music

There will be music there, and song, such music and song as, save in the visions of God, no mortal ear has heard or mind conceived. . . .

The song which the ransomed ones will sing—the song of their experience—will declare the glory of God: "Great and marvelous are Thy works, O Lord God, the Almighty; righteous and true are Thy ways, Thou King of the ages. Who shall not fear, O Lord, and glorify Thy name? for Thou only art holy" [Rev. 15:3, 4, R.V.].—Ed 307-309 (1903).

There is one angel who always leads, who first touches the harp and strikes the note, then all join in the rich, perfect music of heaven. It cannot be described. It is melody, heavenly, divine.—1T 146 (1857).

Not as a man of sorrows, but as a glorious and triumphant king He will stand upon Olivet, while Hebrew hallelujahs mingle with Gentile hosannas, and the voices of the redeemed as a mighty host shall swell the acclamation, Crown Him Lord of all!—DA 830 (1898).

Searching Out the Treasures of the Universe

There, when the veil that darkens our vision shall be removed, and our eyes shall behold that world of beauty of which we now catch glimpses through the microscope, when we look on the glories of the heavens, now scanned afar through the telescope, when, the blight of sin removed, the whole earth shall appear "in the beauty of the Lord our God," what a field will be open to our study! There the student of science may read the records of creation and discern no reminders of the law of evil. He may listen to the music of nature's voices and detect no note of wailing or undertone of sorrow. . . .

All the treasures of the universe will be open to the study of God's children. With unutterable delight we shall enter into the joy and the wisdom of unfallen beings. We shall share the treasures gained through ages upon ages spent in contemplation of God's handiwork.—Ed 303, 307 (1903).

Unfettered by mortality, they wing their tireless flight to worlds afar—worlds that thrilled with sorrow at the spectacle of human woe, and rang with songs of gladness at the tidings of a ransomed soul. . . . With undimmed vision they gaze upon the glory of creation—suns and stars and systems, all in their appointed order circling the throne of Deity. Upon all things, from the least to the greatest, the Creator's name is written, and in all are the riches of His power displayed.—GC 677, 678 (1911).

Sacred History Reviewed

The redeemed throng will range from world to world, and much of their time will be employed in searching out the mysteries of redemption.—7BC 990 (1886).

The themes of redemption will employ the hearts and minds and tongues of the redeemed through the everlasting ages. They will understand the truths which Christ longed to open to His disciples, but which they did not have faith to grasp. Forever and forever new views of the perfection and glory of Christ will appear. Through endless ages will the faithful householder bring forth from his treasure things new and old.—COL 134 (1900).

Then will be opened before him the course of the great conflict that had its birth before time began, and that ends only when time shall cease. The history of the inception of sin, of fatal falsehood in its crooked working, of truth that, swerving not from its own straight lines, has met and conquered error—all will be made manifest. The veil that interposes between the visible and the invisible world will be drawn aside and wonderful things will be revealed. —Ed 304 (1903).

Though the griefs and pains and temptations of earth are ended and the cause removed, the people of God will ever have a distinct, intelligent knowledge of what their salvation has cost. . . .

Our Redeemer will ever bear the marks of His crucifixion. Upon His wounded head, upon His side, His hands and feet, are the only traces of the cruel work that sin has wrought.—GC 651, 674 (1911).

Life's Perplexities Explained

All the perplexities of life's experience will then be made plain. Where to us have appeared only confusion and disappointment, broken purposes and thwarted plans, will be seen a grand, overruling, victorious purpose, a divine harmony.—Ed 305 (1903).

There Jesus will lead us beside the living stream flowing from the throne of God and will explain to us the dark providences through which on this earth He brought us in order to perfect our characters.—8T 254 (1904).

All that has perplexed us in the providences of God will in the world to come be made plain. The things hard to be understood will then find explanation. The mysteries of grace will unfold before us. Where our finite minds discovered only confusion and broken promises, we shall see the most perfect and beautiful harmony. We shall know that infinite love ordered the experiences that seemed most trying. As we realize the tender care of Him who makes all things work together for our good, we shall rejoice with joy unspeakable and full of glory.—9T 286 (1909).

The Outworking of Every Noble Deed

All who have wrought with unselfish spirit will behold the fruit of their labors. The outworking of every right principle and noble deed will be seen. Something of this we see here. But how little of the result of the world's noblest work is in this life manifest to the doer! How many toil unselfishly and unweariedly for those who pass beyond their reach and knowledge! Parents and teachers lie down in their last sleep, their lifework seeming to have been wrought in vain; they know not that their faithfulness has unsealed springs of blessing that can never cease to flow; only by faith they see the children they have trained become a benediction and an inspiration to their fellow men, and the influence repeat itself a thousandfold.

Many a worker sends out into the world messages of strength and hope and courage, words that carry blessing to hearts in every land, but of the results he, toiling in loneliness and obscurity, knows little. So gifts are bestowed, burdens are borne, labor is done. Men sow the seed from which, above their graves, others reap blessed harvests. They plant trees, that others may eat the fruit. They are content here to know that they have set in motion agencies for good. In the hereafter the action and reaction of all these will be seen.—Ed 305, 306 (1903).

Our Joy Will Constantly Increase

There are mysteries in the plan of redemption—the humiliation of the Son of God, that He might be found in fashion as a man, the wonderful love and condescension of the Father in yielding up His Son—that are to the heavenly angels subjects of continual amazement. . . . And these will be the study of the redeemed through eternal ages. As they contemplate the work of God in creation and redemption, new truth will continually unfold to the wondering and delighted mind. As they learn more and more of the wisdom, the love, and the power of God, their minds will be constantly expanding, and their joy will continually increase. —5T 702, 703 (1889).

And the years of eternity, as they roll, will bring richer and still more glorious revelations of God and of Christ. As knowledge is progressive, so will love, reverence, and happiness increase. The more men learn of God, the greater will be their admiration of His character. As Jesus opens before them the riches of redemption and the amazing achievements in the great controversy with Satan, the hearts of the ransomed thrill with more fervent devotion, and with more rapturous joy they sweep the harps of gold; and ten thousand times ten thousand and thousands of thousands of voices unite to swell the mighty chorus of praise.—GC 678 (1911).

Ever an Infinity Beyond

Every power will be developed, every capability increased. The grandest enterprises will be carried forward, the loftiest aspirations will be reached, the highest ambitions realized. And still there will arise new heights to surmount, new wonders to admire, new truths to comprehend, fresh objects to call forth the powers of body and mind and soul.—Ed 307 (1903).

However far we may advance in the knowledge of God's wisdom and His power, there is ever an infinity beyond.—RH Sept. 14, 1886.

All the paternal love which has come down from generation to generation through the channel of human hearts, all the springs of tenderness which have opened in the souls of men, are but as a tiny rill to the boundless ocean when compared with the infinite, exhaustless love of God. Tongue cannot utter it; pen cannot portray it. You may meditate upon it every day of your life; you may search the Scriptures diligently in order to understand it; you may summon every power and capability that God has given you, in the endeavor to comprehend the love and compassion of the heavenly Father; and yet there is an infinity beyond. You may study that love for ages; yet you can never fully comprehend the length and the breadth, the depth and the height, of the love of God in giving His Son to die for the world. Eternity itself can never fully reveal it.—5T 740.

The Whole Universe
Declares That God Is Love

The great controversy is ended. Sin and sinners are no more. The entire universe is clean. One pulse of harmony and gladness beats through the vast creation. From Him who created all, flow life and light and gladness, throughout the realms of illimitable space. From the minutest atom to the greatest world, all things, animate and inanimate, in their unshadowed beauty and perfect joy, declare that God is love.—GC 678 (1911).

SCRIPTURE INDEX

GENERAL INDEX

Adam, ruddy complexion of 291

Angels
  converse with guardian, in heaven 298
  help finish the work 207
  protect God's people in time of trouble 266, 267
  welcome redeemed with singing 281
  will visit people like Cornelius 207

Armageddon, battle of 249-251
  all the world gathered on one side or the other 250
  earth is battlefield for 250
  is battle between good and evil 249, 250
  Jesus leads armies of heaven in 251
  nations held in check until 239
  providence has part in 251

Atmosphere, poisoned by Satan 26, 27

B

Babylon, fall of,
  completed by universal Sunday legislation 198
  not yet complete 198

Bible, *see* Scriptures

Blessings, must not forget past 72

Brethren of experience, submit new ideas to 91

C

Calamities
  God's purpose in, 27, 28
  Sabbathkeepers blamed for 257

Chicago, caution concerning 113

313

will pass Sunday law
128, 129
will repudiate Consti-
tution 131
Unity, importance of
91, 92
Universe, inhabitants of,
approve God's actions
30
declare that God is
love 306
are watching this
earth 30

V

Voice of God, the
Battle Creek no
longer 50
church speaks as 47,
56
General Conference
no longer 50

gives day and hour of
Christ's return 272
God's people de-
livered at 269

W

**Waggoner and Jones,
Elders,** brought
precious message 200
Waymarks should be
studied 14
Wicked, destruction of,
an act of mercy 279,
280
Worldlings
not to confederate
with 84
not to mingle with,
for pleasure 85
Worship, family,
short and spirited 83,
84